Speak for Millions

How to Make
REALLY BIG MONEY
as a
Professional
Speaker

FRED GLEECK

— First Edition —

Fast Forward Press • Henderson, NV

Speaking for Millions

How to Make Really Big Money as a Professional Speaker

by Fred Gleeck

Published by:

Fast Forward Press
209 Horizon Peak Drive
Henderson, NV 89012
702-617-4205 – phone
fgleeck@aol.com
www.fastforwardpress.com

Cover design and interior layout © TLC Graphics,
www.TLCGraphics.com

Copyright © 2002 by Fred Gleeck

ISBN # (0-936965-03-7)

LCCN Number: 00-104117

CIP Data Block

Contact Information/ Our Web Site

I would love to hear from you. Your questions, your comments, any and all are welcome. Don't be a stranger. My contact information is listed below and I encourage you to contact me in whatever way is easiest for you.

I am also available for speaking engagements on a wide variety of topics. Call for details.

My email address is fgleeck@aol.com.

My phone number is 702-617-4205.

My mailing address is:
Fred Gleeck
209 Horizon Peak Drive, Suite 202
Henderson, NV 89012
www.professionalspeakingsuccess.com

This site is dedicated to helping anyone make more money as a professional speaker. Whether you're a veteran speaker or just getting started, this site is for you. You'll learn the latest information to help catapult your speaking business into the stratosphere.

Tips@professionalspeakingsuccess.com

If you would like to receive speaking tips via email on a regular basis, please go to this Web address and sign up. You will then receive periodic tips about how to improve your speaking business.

Acknowledgements

I would like to acknowledge a number of people who have been very helpful in the preparation of this book.

I thank Tami Dever and Erin Stark at TLC Graphics (www.tlcgraphics.com) for their AMAZING cover design. It captures the exact feel that I wanted. They also did a great job in designing the interior of this book — it works extremely well with the cover itself.

The printing of this and all of my books is being done by Quest Print. Their efforts are much appreciated. You can reach Tim Swope by calling 866-947-8378, ext. 239. Make sure to tell him I sent you. Also, if you wish to purchase this book in quantity, you can do so by calling Tim directly. I have authorized him to sell you the book at cost.

I thank my mentor (now deceased), Howard Shenson for his time, friendship and advice. If not for him, I'd probably NOT be a professional speaker.

In my opinion, the best speaker on the planet (other than myself) is Lou Heckler. Thank you, Lou, for being who you are! You're a great example of what a professional speaker should be.

If you do find any errors in this book, they're here for a purpose. Some people actually like looking for them and we strive to please as many people as possible. If you find any typos or grammatical errors, please email them to me at fgleeck@aol.com. If you send me a number of them I will reward you with a small gift — unless you find so many of them that I feel you deserve a large gift.

Contents

My Background

My name is Fred Gleeck and I have been speaking professionally for more than seventeen years. I got started as a speaker in a similar way that many of you are doing right now; I read a book. The book was called: "Put Your Money Where Your Mouth Is" by Robert Anthony. I had seen an ad for the book in *Success* magazine and ordered it.

I read that book in 1979 right after finishing up my Masters Degree in International Business. When I finished the book, I knew it was only a matter of time before I made speaking my profession.

I had always enjoyed getting up in front of groups and speaking. It was reinforced when I was on the "speakers committee" in graduate school. We were responsible for booking outside speakers.

The first speaker that I had a hand in booking was Richard Valeriani. At the time he was an NBC News correspondent. I was chosen to introduce him. Even getting up to introduce a speaker in front of a large group of my peers I found very exciting. After I saw him give his speech I was convinced that speaking was for me.

Later that year I had to do a presentation in front of 500 people. I found that even more exhilarating. I had done some theatre in high school and liked being a "ham." Chances are many of you have had similar experiences.

I also suspect I gravitated towards speaking because my Dad used to send my letters back from college corrected in red pen. I couldn't compete with him as a writer, but, I was much better than he was as a speaker.

When I got out of graduate school I moved to New York City where I was promptly fired from five Fortune 500 companies in a row. There seemed to be unanimous agreement that I should be self-employed. It took me five years to finally get into the profession where I knew I belonged: SPEAKING.

I gave my first paid presentation when I promoted one of my own seminars on "How to Start Your Own Consulting Business." That was in May of 1984.

I promoted the seminar using newspaper ads (two large display ads on successive Sundays). I charged $95 for the seminar and made $2000 in profit on a Saturday in Saddlebrook, New Jersey. If I had been smart enough to have product to sell, I would have made a good bit more. The very next time I spoke I did have products to sell. This signficantly increased my speaking income.

Years later, I joined the largest public seminar company (at the time) called CareerTrack. You may have heard of them. I was with them for four years. I was their top rated speaker in each of my topics all four years. The two areas in which they rated us were on customer satisfaction with the seminars themselves and the product sales numbers. I had the highest numbers in all my topics in both areas.

This served as a great training ground. Like an actor doing a LOT of Off-Broadway work, I worked many of the second and third tier cities. While I was there I very much enjoyed it, but it was a lot work for very little money.

I now speak an average of 90 - 100 times a year to groups around the country and around the world (on a limited basis - my choice). Many of these speaking engagements are self-promoted seminars.

I consider myself to be a very good speaker, but I am even better in the area of product development and product sales. As it turns out, this is an area that has helped me make the bulk of my money in the speaking business. This is true with most highly successful professional speakers. I will share all my secrets with you throughout the book.

The only other item that people usually want to know is my educational background. I have an undergraduate degree in Marketing and Psychology and a masters' degree in International Business.

From my experience in the speaking field, education is virtually meaningless to your success as a speaker. So, don't feel like you have to go out and get an education before you get started. Nothing could be further from the truth.

Warning – Disclaimer

This book is designed to help you learn and profit from the speaking business in the shortest amount of time possible.

Every effort has been made to give you information which is 100% accurate. Mistakes, however, may have been made along the way, and for that, I am sorry.

The information in this book is no guarantee that you will succeed as a speaker, even if you follow all the techniques described. There are too many intangibles for me to suggest that everyone who reads this will be successful.

The system described in this book with give you the GREATEST possible chance for success. Once again, no guarantees can be made about your particular ability to succeed. What I can say for certain is that many people have used my system to become highly successful professional speakers.

This book, therefore cannot <u>guarantee</u> your success.

If you do not wish to be bound by the above, you may return the book to the publisher for a full refund.

"A wise man is he who knows he knows not."
— SOCRATES —

Introduction

If you love getting up in front of people and speaking, why not do it for a living? It's possible, but you need to read this book to make sure you have the greatest probability of success.

There are a number of books out on the market that give you advice on how to get into the business of making money as a speaker. How is this one different?

Very simple. This is the straight story from someone who has been there. No BS. No theory. Just simple, practical ideas to show you how to make big money as a professional speaker.

I'm here to break the "code of silence." To tell you what others won't tell you. To give you the inside story. To tell you the whole truth. You will not find this information in any other book on the topic.

This book will get a lot of people annoyed. It's going to get speakers bureaus pissed off. For the most part, these folks are overpriced opportunists who aren't worth what they are paid. There are a select FEW who don't fall into that category!

I'm also going to get my fellow speakers annoyed. Many of these folks are pompous and pretentious jerks who strut around thinking they are rock stars. Trust me, they are not!

The reason speakers are going to be annoyed with me is there are a lot of "dirty little secrets" in the speaking business that no one talks about. I'm going to spill the beans. I'm going to give you the information that few people ever discuss.

Speaking can be an incredible business. It can be a lot of fun and very financially rewarding, but you need a roadmap to get to the top as quickly as possible. This book is designed to help you cut through the crap and get to the pot of gold quickly and easily.

Other books on the topic will give you some clever ideas, but only this one will give you a specific roadmap to success as a speaker that anyone can follow.

Remember, just because there is a book on a topic, it doesn't mean the information is accurate or correct. There are a number of books out on the topic of professional speaking. Needless to say there is a LOT of misinformation. The system in this book works. I know because it is working for me and for my many clients.

My Goals for You and for Myself

I think it would be a good idea to share with you what my goals are as a speaker. Remember, these are **my** goals. They may or not be similar to your own.

First, I want to net $1,000,000 a year without any employees. I want to be able to operate the business without the hassles (in my opinion) of having someone work for me. I MAY want to have an assistant at some point, but it will depend on how good a person I can find for the job.

With this money I will give a large portion of it to causes that I believe in.

I will do this by generating money from 6 primary sources. These include speaking engagements, seminars (self promoted and those of others), consulting, coaching, products and websites.

Second, I want to have three residences. Currently I have two, one here in the Las Vegas area and one in New York City. Eventually I want to have a third residence in Europe. My plan is to spend November to April in Las Vegas, Spring in New York City, Summer in Europe and Fall back in New York.

My goal for YOU is to help you make as much money as possible in the shortest period of time as a professional speaker. How you spend that money is up to you.

Getting Started

My System

My system for generating speaking engagements is VERY different than just about all of my colleagues. The vast majority of speakers go after speaking engagements directly. They either try to get booked for speeches directly (going to meeting planners) or they curry favor with speakers bureaus in hopes that they'll get booked.

Both of these methodologies will cost you money and time. As is true with most business models, your marketing is a cost center.

The system that I want you to pursue as your primary means of getting business makes your marketing efforts a profit center. How can this be?

Simple.

I take a niche market and develop a line of products that range in price from $10 to $1000. These products include books, ebooks, audios, CD-roms, DVDs, videos, seminars, teleseminars, workshops and bootcamps.

I then create a web-based system to sell these products and sequentially trade people up to higher and higher priced products.

How does this generate speaking engagements?

A certain percentage of people who you feed into the top of your funnel in any of your niche markets will eventually use you as a speaker. Here's an example. One of my markets is the self storage industry. I have a whole line of products that I've developed to help these folks generate more business. Not long ago, someone read one of my articles in a trade magazine. They signed up for my regular tips that I send to people on a regular basis.

Fred Gleeck's Funnel System

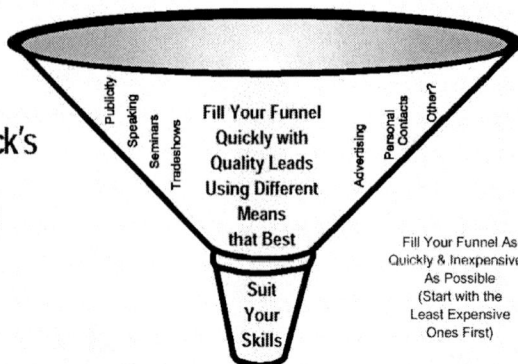

Fill Your Funnel Quickly with Quality Leads Using Different Means that Best Suit Your Skills

Publicity · Speaking · Seminars · Tradeshows · Advertising · Personal Contacts · Other?

Fill Your Funnel As Quickly & Inexpensively As Possible (Start with the Least Expensive Ones First)

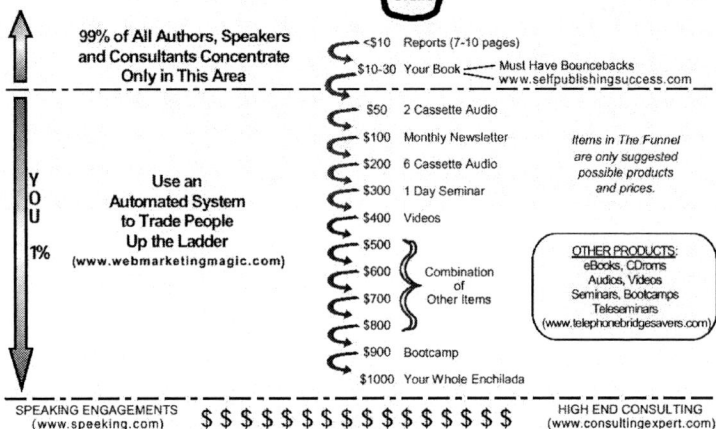

99% of All Authors, Speakers and Consultants Concentrate Only in This Area

YOU 1%

Use an Automated System to Trade People Up the Ladder (www.webmarketingmagic.com)

Price	Item
<$10	Reports (7-10 pages)
$10-30	Your Book — Must Have Bouncebacks www.selfpublishingsuccess.com
$50	2 Cassette Audio
$100	Monthly Newsletter
$200	6 Cassette Audio
$300	1 Day Seminar
$400	Videos
$500	
$600	Combination of Other Items
$700	
$800	
$900	Bootcamp
$1000	Your Whole Enchilada

Items in The Funnel are only suggested possible products and prices.

OTHER PRODUCTS: eBooks, CDroms Audios, Videos Seminars, Bootcamps Teleseminars (www.telephonebridgesavers.com)

SPEAKING ENGAGEMENTS (www.speeking.com)

$ $ $ $ $ $ $ $ $ $ $ $ $ $ $

HIGH END CONSULTING (www.consultingexpert.com)

Your Holy Grail: Capture the Greatest Number of Opt-In Emails

YOU Can Make DOUBLE or TRIPLE What the Average Author/Speaker/Consultant Makes!

In this particular example, this individual bought my book for $99 which I offered in my 4th email message to him. After buying a few videos a few weeks later I got a call at my office. He wanted to know my rates to come to Hawaii and do 3 days of training/speaking for his staff.

Had I tried to go after this customer without the system I've described above I would have spent money in marketing to him. In my system, I MAKE money while I'm marketing my speaking and consulting services.

In this day and age, every speaker is not just a speaker. They are authors, consultants and product developers as well. In short, speakers are INFORMATION MARKETERS.

I'm not saying that you use the system that I've described exclusively. I am saying that you should start testing this system in a targeted niche market. This will show you how the system works and how you can turn your marketing efforts into a profit center.

If you need my help in setting it up, just give me a call.

Beginning Speaker Tips

Success as a speaker is more related to your marketing abilities than your speaking abilities. Sad, but true. But to be perfectly honest, you need both.

If you are just starting out as a speaker, here are some things you need to do. If you follow these suggestions you will be on your way to a lucrative speaking career.

Read Aloud

Pull a book off the shelf each night and read aloud for a minimum of 15 to 20 minutes. The only way to get better as a speaker is to practice. If you can't practice in front of a live audience, then practice on your own. Even with the greatest marketing skills you still need to do a great job when you get up in front of a group. Reading aloud will help you to improve your "instrument."

Start Writing

Similar to speaking, the only way to improve your writing skills is to write. I have a goal to write a minimum of 5,000 words a day. The only way to get better as a writer is to practice. If you learn how to write, it will dramatically help your speaking career. How? Simple. Speakers who have books written on their topics of expertise make substantially more money than those who don't. My research indicates that speakers who have books generally make close to double the money than those who don't.

If you aren't a great writer, don't worry. You can always hire a great editor. If you can't write at all you can also hire a ghost writer. I have no moral objection to this at all. As long as the ideas are yours, that's all that matters!

Go to Toastmasters

Toastmasters is an organization that will help you perfect your speaking skills. They can help the new speaker to learn some of the speaking basics. They have a workbook and an agenda for any new speaker to go through. I highly recommend this group if you are just starting out as a speaker. It won't make you an expert speaker, but it will help get you started in the right direction. Toastmasters have local branches all over the country. You can find the closest branch by visiting their website at: www.toastmasters.org.

Watch Other Speakers

Another great way to learn how to speak better is to watch others who are experts in the field. Find those speakers who you like and dissect their speeches. What do they do that makes you feel positive about them? Don't copy them, but adapt their methodologies into your own personal style of delivery.

Go to Seminars

Attend seminars on how to better market your speaking business and career. I offer a number of these for beginning speakers. It's a good idea to take these seminars for not just the content, but also for the contacts. NEVER attend a seminar that doesn't offer you a money back guarantee.

Start Speaking

Speak anytime, anywhere, for free if necessary. Well, not really for free. I'll explain that later.

Top 5 ways that speakers get their business

As you go through this book, you need to keep in mind that speakers get their business in five primary ways. This will give you a blueprint for how you should run your marketing efforts. Concentrate your efforts in the order in which they are presented here. Don't concentrate on number five until you've completely exhausted your efforts in the first four. These steps are in this order for a reason. Don't try to reinvent the wheel. You'll be wasting your time.

1   Someone Heard the Speaker: Speak anytime/anywhere for free if necessary

The best and least costly means of marketing yourself as a speaker is to have someone hear you and decide that you'd be perfect to speak for their group. A number of years back, I bumped into a guy on a plane. We got to talking. He told me he was traveling to go to an industry convention. I told him I was going to that particular city to give a speech (to a different convention).

I invited him to come here me speak. He did. The following year his group used me for a keynote at their convention. At that same event I had another person come up to me after I spoke and request a business card. Later that year I spoke to his organization.

The lesson? Speak anywhere, anytime, for free if you have to. The more people who see you, the greater the number of requests you will get to speak. Provided that you do a great job!

2   Referral: Always be good, even if there are 5 people there

For this to work you have to do a great job EVERY time you speak. Make sure you do a great job regardless of how many people there are in the room. Remember, all you have to do is impress ONE of them each time you speak to keep this system going forever.

3   Celebrity: People gain celebrity status as the result of writing a book

You're going to have to write a book if you're going to make a lot of money as a speaker. If this sounds scary, don't worry! I've developed a system that will get your book written, printed and have it start getting sold in less than 90 days. Yes, that's right! In less than 3 months from today you can have a book ready to sell. The book will also become your best piece of promotional material. If you can't wait to read about this system, go to: www.selfpublishingsuccess.com.

4   Industry Expert: Gain a reputation in a niche market

You're much more apt to get speaking engagements if you're perceived as an expert in the field. Being a generalist is poor positioning for all but the very well known, celebrity speakers. I encourage you to take your area of expertise and NICHE IT into one or more markets where you have a natural match or interest.

This will mean that you write articles for their trade publications and speak and/or exhibit at all of their trade shows.

5   Speaker Promotional Materials: 1 page faxable, tiered brochure, demo video, web

This is where most speakers spend the bulk of their efforts. Inappropriately, I might add. Notice that this is number five on the list. Concentrate on the first four elements first. That's not to say that you shouldn't have or create promotional materials, but don't concentrate your efforts in this area alone.

These are the top five ways that speakers get their business. You'll learn more about each of these as you go through this book. Don't worry, it's all here.

Are You a Motivational Speaker?

This is a question that I get asked all the time. Whenever you tell someone that you speak for a living, their inevitable next question is: Are you a motivational speaker? My answer is usually: "No, I'm more of an informational speaker who is highly motivating."

I answer this way because I have an innate discomfort with this classification. To me the term "motivational speaker" conjures up a speaker that delivers a lot of feel good catch phrases and very little content. For those of you who watch Saturday Night Live, the character that Chris Farley used to portray. I equate these kinds of speakers with a Chinese food meal. You're usually still hungry after you've heard them speak.

Many years ago I was on the platform with a gold medal Olympian. I watched as this well known individual did her speech. I found myself completely unimpressed. Then I watched as the throngs of audience members came up to this person saying how much they loved her talk. I was amazed.

This proves a very important point. **You** are not your audience. Don't ever assume that you act, think, or even behave like the members of your audience. Clearly, from the above example, I was out of touch.

I think I'm probably out of touch with regards to how I feel about most "motivational" speakers. I personally don't like these kinds of speakers. Please don't take this the wrong way if this is the kind of speaker you want to be. I want you to be more than just a motivational speaker.

There is obviously plenty of demand for this type of speaker, they just aren't my cup of tea. But I think I am ahead of the curve on this issue and have a warning for those of you positioning yourself this way. In addition to being a motivational speaker, you better find a way to deliver valuable content as well. If you don't, your speaking career will be short-lived.

In the very near future, audiences will demand not just motivation, but motivation with a message.

Another problem with being a motivational speaker is that you aren't niched. It makes you a generalist. Being a generalist makes it tougher to be sold to a client.

Categorizing yourself as a motivational speaker will make the pool of competitors much larger than speakers who have a more specific topic orientation.

Speak to Any Group, Any Time, If You Are Available

One of the keys to speaking success is to do a lot of speaking. How do you get started if you have limited experience? Speak any time, anywhere, and for free if you must.

By free, I don't really mean totally for free. I mean that you don't charge them a fee for speaking. But if you are speaking for free, they must allow you to sell your products. Depending on the group you are speaking to, the products you select to offer will vary.

One of my first speeches was for a local service organization. They didn't give me a fee but allowed me to sell a one cassette program for $20 a piece. I sold 22 of them. Total revenue of $440. Cost of production? $20. They cost about $1 each. Total net revenue? $420. Not bad for a beginner with a 45 minute speech. They also gave me a "wonderful" chicken dinner.

You'll get resistance from people where you offer to speak for free because they've had bad experiences in the past. Many of these folks have had people come in to give a free speech and used their 45 minutes to deliver an extended sales pitch for their products and services. So, don't be surprised if you encounter some resistance.

You get around this by letting them know that you will deliver a lot of content and only BRIEFLY pitch your products at the end.

The reason why you want to speak for free in the beginning is that you need to practice, and the more you practice the better you'll get.

The more people who see you, the better it is for you as well. The goal is to start building your database. Find a way to get people to give you their email addresses. The main thing you want to do when you start speaking is build a database of people who have heard you speak. Your database will become your single greatest asset.

The people who see and hear you at these early events will stay on your database forever and may buy more "stuff" from you over the years.

One of my biggest mistakes as a speaker (early on) was not meticulously capturing the names of my audience members. I didn't start keeping my database until years after I started speaking. This cost me (as a guess) a minimum of $100,000 during my early years.

When you do a speech, make sure to give participants a handout. Make it something worth keeping. Not only will your message be more effective, it will also serve to keep your name in front of the participants well after the event is over.

Your handout should both serve to keep your name in front of people (make sure to put your contact info on every page) and to make people an offer that will capture their email address. When I'm giving my speech or seminar on seminar marketing I put on the bottom of the handout a way for people to get a free 7-day course on the topic that normally costs $77. All they have to do is email me at that address and they get it for free. I encourage YOU to send an email to tips@seminarexpert.com to learn more about the topic as well.

Make sure you have your name and contact information on every page of every handout you distribute. If someone makes copies, you'll want people to know where it came from.

So stop waiting for paid speaking engagements and start speaking anywhere and everywhere you possibly can.

BEING YOURSELF AND DEVELOPING YOUR UNIQUE STYLE

Your personal style when you do your speech or seminar is important. Most important is that you don't violate the rule of being yourself. My style is very strong and confrontational. Yours may be different. Don't try to be like me or anyone else. Try to be the absolute best you, you can be.

There is a strong tendency on the part of new speakers to copy people they hear who they like. Avoid this temptation. Try to learn from those you like, but don't imitate them. It will come off as fake.

Build your own style by taking the best of what you see from others and combining it into a powerful hybrid of your own.

People can smell baloney. Don't try to be something that you're not. It won't work. People will judge you as a phoney.

The best two success examples I can give you for being yourself would be Hugh Downs and Oprah Winfrey. In my opinion, the reason for the success of these two TV personalities is the result of their coming across as 100% authentic and real.

Audiences respond to this approach.

My style will sometimes get people angry. I tend to be very direct and "in your face" on occasion. I am willing to risk alienating a very small percentage of the audience if I feel that I can best deliver my content and information in this manner.

You have to make your choices, but keep in mind that the more people get the feeling that you are authentic, the better your evaluations and product sales will be. We'll talk more about how to do this later in the book.

Start Local

Like every speaker, your goal is to be speaking to thousands of people every time you speak, both from an ego gratification and a money standpoint. But to get there you have to start somewhere. Very few speakers, unless they have just won an Olympic Gold Medal, can go from complete novice to the top ranks overnight.

You have to start local. Go to your local Rotary, Lions, Elks and other service clubs and offer to speak to them for free. You will usually get at least a chicken lunch or dinner for your efforts. Just because it's a local organization doesn't mean you shouldn't still give it your best effort. Those Rotarians and others often own companies who can use trainers or speakers.

Make sure that the groups will allow you to make your products available for sale.

Remember to start local and then expand outward from your home base in a series of concentric circles. Don't worry about trying to get to travel; you'll have plenty of that soon enough.

Your action point is to go to your yellow pages in your local community and look under the heading: ASSOCIATIONS. Call them all up and try to get them to let you speak. Don't be discouraged if they are booked a few months in advance. Take the first open slot and work on other things in the interim.

Developing Your Speaking Image

What kind of image are you trying to develop? If you can't answer that question you need to think about an answer. The formation of an image is an important element of your marketing plan and strategy.

Successful speakers almost always have an image. Some have cultivated it in a cold and calculating manner. Others have developed one without making the effort. If you can, try to carefully construct and create your own.

The person that immediately pops into my head when I think of an image is a "veteran" speaker named Charlie "Tremendous" Jones. He is a big bear of a guy with a huge heart. If you hadn't met him in person, you would think he was a fake.

Whenever he sees someone, whether he knows them or not, he runs up to them and gives them this huge bear hug.

He is one of these ultra-enthusiastic speakers who is primarily a motivator. He doesn't give out a lot of content, but you leave an event where he has spoken feeling energized. Although I'm not normally a fan of this kind of speaker, he is someone I like a whole lot.

My goal is to cultivate the image of a high content, but very entertaining speaker on topics of marketing and other closely related issues. I also want to cultivate an image of a speaker who isn't a prima donna and will roll with the punches when there is a problem.

What image are you shooting for? Start thinking about it now!

Being Different as a Speaker

Some speakers go the route of adopting the persona of a historical character. This has worked out very well for a number of professional speakers. One I know portrays Ben Franklin, another plays Albert Einstein and the list goes on from there.

If you feel passionate about a particular character from history, I wouldn't dissuade you from going this route. Only do it if you have a great deal of passion for a particular person.

There are a number of other ways that you can choose to be different as a speaker. Some people wear odd shaped glasses or different color shoes. However, I would rather you make your mark as a great speaker, not as a clown.

What's Your USP?

Closely attached to the issue of image is deciding on what your UNIQUE SELLING PROPOSITION is as a speaker.

What do you bring to the table as a speaker that no one else has? When I used to do a lot of speeches on customer service, I was just one of many possible speakers on that topic who my potential clients could choose from.

What would happen is a client would say they wanted someone to talk about customer service issues. Perhaps they were dealing with two or possibly even three speakers bureaus. Within the client's budget they would then be sent videos from the top five people that each bureau had to recommend.

Even assuming that two of the speakers sent by all the bureaus were the same, the meeting planner still had to look at thirteen separate videos to decide on a speaker for that topic. I personally don't like these odds. And neither should you.

How to combat these odds?

Put yourself into a position where you combine image and topic expertise and become a unique entity.

One of the best ways to do this is to target specific industries and gain expertise in the industry. As an example, when someone wants a speaker on marketing who has knowledge of the financial service area, I am one of the few who comes to mind.

If they are looking for an expert in marketing in the SELF STORAGE industry, I'm their guy. After all, I wrote the book on self storage marketing and speak at all of the industry conventions.

So to develop a USP you need to concentrate on two areas. First, in the area of topic: try to find a topic that you are both passionate about and where there aren't 2,000 speakers who have chosen the same topic. Also, pick a few industries to specialize in. Make sure those industries are broad enough to give you the opportunity for getting plenty of speaking work.

The goal is to make it so you have NO competition when competing for a speaking engagement. The best way to do this is to write a book on your topic which is specific to a given industry.

My example would be my book called "Secrets of Self Storage Marketing Success." If someone wants someone to speak on marketing as it relates to the storage industry, my name is on a VERY short list.

My problem, in this example, is two-fold. First, self storage is a very narrow market. Second, once they have used me as a speaker a few times, they want someone new.

The solution is two-fold for me. Keep adding markets, and keep writing more niche specific books.

Use my example to decide what you need to do.

Setting Your Goals as a Speaker

The story is told of the guy who wants to take a trip. He goes to the airport. When he gets to the airline counter he approaches the ticket agent. He says: "I'd like a ticket."

The ticket agent asks him where he wants to go. He says: "I'm not quite sure." The agent then follows up with the question, "When do you want to leave?" He responds: "I'm not sure of that either."

It is clear that this individual is going one place: NOWHERE!

Unless you have some very specific goals for your speaking business, the chances of achieving maximum success are minimal. The big questions for you will be defining what success is to you. It will be different for everyone.

The first step is to decide what it is you truly want.

You will hear a lot of speakers pay a lot of lip service as to how they want to "help change lives." Granted, you will hopefully touch a lot of peoples' hearts. To be honest, whenever I hear speakers talking this way it sounds incredibly disingenuous. You get the feeling that they say these things more because they are <u>supposed</u> to than because they truly mean it.

Whatever your goals, you need to first make sure that they are your own, that your goals have not been established by your parents, your spouse, or anyone else whom you are trying to please. How do you do this? I have to be honest, I really don't know.

But probably the best way is to visualize yourself already achieving the goal that you set for yourself and see how you feel. Does it feel right? Does it feel good? Are you happy when you picture this?

Get a hold of a Brian Tracy program on goal setting. This will help you attain your goals as a speaker much more quickly. Another option is to come to one of my speaking bootcamps. You'll find more information about the bootcamp and other seminars at the back of the book.

My goal is to NET $1,000,000 a year without any employees. What's yours?

Naming Your Speaking Company

People do a lot of obsessing about what to name their speaking/consulting company. Keep it simple for the best results.

I made a big mistake when I first got started. I decided that I needed to give my speaking business a fancy name. I came up with "Growth Resources." This was a big mistake. Not only because of the name, but because I incorporated before I should have. Refer to the section on speaker finances for more information on that issue.

My organization is now called Fred Gleeck Productions. I suggest you come up with something similar. Use your name when you name your speaking business. That way, when you get good press, it will accrue to you directly, and not some nebulous organization like Growth Resources.

So make sure to use your name when you name your speaking business. Many speakers will disagree with me. Some call their organizations the blah, blah, blah institute. I think that this looks like you are taking yourself altogether too seriously.

Maybe it's just a matter of style, but I think your clients are suitably unimpressed by this attempt to elevate yourself and your organization by using a pretentious name.

Keeping Your Books as a Speaker

I have a very important recommendation to give you here. Don't try to do your own taxes. Leave that to an expert. I have been working with someone for years who I trust. His is the only name that I give out at seminars or put into print. His name is Chris Trinka. His number is 212-628-3139.

No matter where you are located, he can work with you. He works with a lot of my friends and clients. In addition to that, he knows speakers and how their businesses work.

In order to save you money when you go to Chris or any accountant, do the following: first, make a copy of every check that comes in, then attach a copy of that check or checks to the deposit ticket you get from the bank when you make a deposit.

Second, on the deposit ticket where the money came from, write the name of the client and what the money was for.

Finally, every month take all of your deposit tickets and summarize the deposits to let you know exactly where your money came from.

On the expense side, I highly recommend that you use just one credit card for business purposes, preferably a platinum card so they will give you a summary at the end of the year.

Take any and all cash receipts and immediately write the date on them and what the expense was for. When you get home, have one place where you keep receipts. Then summarize them at the end of the month and put them into an envelope.

The Benefits of Low Fixed Overhead

If you want my one secret to speaking success that has nothing to do with speaking itself, here it is. Keep your overhead low.

If you can easily pay all of your bills each month without having to do a lot of work, here is what will happen.

People will call you to do a speaking engagement. When you talk to them over the phone you will not sound desperate.

The net result?

You will get more work. It just seems to be a law of nature that the more you push something, the harder it pushes back. Just think about dating. Someone who is desperate for a date rarely gets one. Case closed.

The people on the other side of the phone will hear a confident you, rather than a desperate you. Which of these two types would you prefer to do business with?

So forget the fancy sports cars. Drive a Honda like I do. Forget the $900 suits; shop for bargains like I do. Simplify your life and keep your overhead low. It will cut your budget and your stress level. And on top of it all, you'll land more speaking engagements.

Office Tools for Speakers

There are some basic tools that you must have at your office as a speaker.

Phone

Pick up a phone that has some key features. First and foremost you need a good speaker phone attached. Not that you will use the speaker phone to speak to people, but so that when you are on hold you will be able to put the phone down and go about your other work until the other party picks up. This saves you a lot of time and neck pain.

Also, have a headset that you can attach to the phone. I like the ones that have a portable phone and a headset attachment. That way you can walk all over the place without getting tangled in cords and still make use of a headset.

I highly recommend that you take a look at the Panasonic phones. They are the only large phone vendor who I can recommend.

Fax

A fax machine is an essential element of your office tools. You need one because it is still one of the primary means of communication.

Some people will claim that you don't need to have a fax machine because we have email and all sorts of other web related items. Baloney. You need to have a fax machine to both send and receive faxes. If you can't get a real fancy one to start don't worry, get a cheap one. It will cost you no more than $150.

Email

You should have an email address specifically for your speaking business. I still use AOL. Yes, for you computer geeks, I know they suck. BUT, many people are still using them. I like the idea of having an AOL address and another address. I also recommend that you separate your business correspondence from your personal correspondence.

Consider using one of the free email providers. Your chances of getting a virus are significantly reduced.

If you are dealing with multiple niche markets like I do, you may want to have separate email addresses for each one so you know which market they are inquiring about.

Website

You need a web site as a speaker. If you don't want to spend a lot of money initially, you can go to bigyellow.com and put together a free site.

Eventually you will want to get and establish your own domain name with your web site. As a minimum, go to godaddy.com and reserve yourname.com. This will make it so that you will always have one place where people can find you. Make sure to reserve some of the standard Mis-spellings as well.

In addition to fredgleeck.com, I have numerous other specific web domains for each of my market niches like selfstoragesuccess.com.

Wall Calendar

There is nothing worse than having a potential client call and not knowing whether or not you are booked on a given day. The best way to make sure this doesn't happen is to use a large wall calendar. This way you can quickly and easily see if a given date is available.

Depending on how far along you are in your career, you may need to have multiple years up on the wall. I have the current year, the last year and next year's calendar on the wall in my office. For dates any further into the future I keep a book that is marked "Future Dates." This is for all dates that are past the end of next year for which I don't have a wall calendar up.

Master Calendar/Assistant Calendar

You need to have a master calendar that you carry around with you as well. I keep it in my Franklin Planner. If you get any bookings while you are out of the office, make sure to transfer them from your planner onto the wall calendar at your office.

If you work with an assistant, be certain that your calendars are in sync. There is nothing worse than agreeing to an engagement and finding out that you are double booked. I have made myself look like a knucklehead on numerous occasions. Don't make the mistakes I did.

Filing System

There are many people out there who are bigger experts than I am on organization. My filing system is simple. Any active file is placed on top of my desk in a file holder. By active file I mean anything that I am working on right now.

For any speaking event, I have a file in the office which contains all files of speaking events that are at any stage other than completed. If they call and I send out a contract, a file is created and put in this area. In the front of each folder is a checklist and the files are put in alphabetical order.

If a client with an upcoming speaking engagement calls, I look through this filing area and will quickly find them by their name.

The only problem with this system is that the checklist is inside each of the folders. I review each folder every morning to see if anything needs to be done that day or week that is on the checklist within a folder. This may seem like a lot of work, but it only takes ten minutes each day. It also serves as a great review for me.

Looking through the files everyday will make it so I know, almost without looking, who needs what and when.

Whether you follow this system or one that you create for yourself, have a system of some sort or you'll go completely insane.

Answering Machines

Everyone these days either uses an answering machine or some form of voice mail. It is very unusual that you can actually speak to a physical human being these days when you call anywhere. People accept this fact. What they don't accept is not getting their phone calls returned in a timely manner. This is, and should be, unacceptable.

Make yourself a promise to return all calls within 24 hours after you receive them. Preferably, the same day. I remember waiting 48 hours to return a phone call a number of years back. It cost me a very lucrative speaking engagement.

If you can't return the call yourself and you have an assistant, have them call the person back to let them know you are traveling or otherwise indisposed. This is just common courtesy as well as good business practice.

Also, if you can get in the habit (I haven't been able to), change your message on your machine every day. This lets people know you are very voice mail conscious and will make them even more confident of leaving a message. If you start this practice, you have to keep doing it. There is nothing worse than getting someone's voice mail which refers to a vacation that they are supposedly on over Memorial Day when you are calling after Labor Day.

As it relates to leaving your own messages on other people's voice mail, remember, you are a speaker and the way you leave a message will count.

Make it clear and well spoken. Keep it short and concise, explaining exactly who you are, why you are calling and what you would like them to do. Never expect them to have your number, always leave it as part of your message when you call.

Toll Free Numbers

In answer to the question of whether or not you should spend the money to have a toll free number, the answer is YES! I have had my 800 number, 1-800-FGLEECK for years. The largest monthly bill I can ever remember was around $150.

Here is why I think you should invest in one. First, the cost is minimal given what can happen as a result. Let me give you two examples. A year and a half after I gave a speech for a company, I got a call from someone who had been at the event. They remembered my last name and remembered that my toll free number was related to my name.

Tough to forget a fairly weird last name like Gleeck. The lady who called had moved from one company (where she heard me speak) to another one. She called 1-800-FGLEECK and I had a speaking engagement for $3500. That should pay the cost of the 800 number for a few years! Get a toll-free number and you will, on occasion, have something similar happen to you.

The other reason why I like having a toll-free number is peoples' perceptions. Even though everyone knows that having an 800/888/877 number is fairly cheap, they still expect a true professional to have one. Having a toll-free number will impress only your friends and relatives, but it is mandatory to your clients to look like you are "for real."

The number of toll free numbers is dwindling fast. I am glad that I have an 800 number and not an 888 or 877. It shows a certain amount of longevity. If you want a particular 800 number, call it. You may be able to "acquire" the number for a fee from the current owner. If this is too expensive, get some kind of a toll free number, regardless of which one it is.

Make sure to talk to Matt Stracner at Zirvo Communications to get the best rates on 800 numbers and standard long distance. His number is 800-447-9476. Tell him I sent you.

Working with Other Professionals

Many speakers try to be their own graphic designer, copywriter, and just about everything else.

If there is one very important lesson I have learned as a speaker it is to hire people to do things that you aren't an expert at yourself. First off, your time is better spent trying to generate speaking and product income.

Second, you will probably do a poor and highly inefficient job at these other tasks.

Compute how much money per hour you make as a speaker. Now compare that fee to how much you have to pay someone to do the work you really shouldn't be doing yourself. In actuality, the services you are buying are pretty darn cheap.

In the beginning, if you don't have the money to pay others for their services, try to barter with them for something where you have expertise. Don't try to go out and learn a whole new field; it won't be worth your time or money.

My web sites aren't as good as I'd like them to be. Should I now go out and try to learn how to create web sites? No. Although I might be tempted to save a few bucks, I'll find someone who knows how to do them and hire them, instead.

This will allow me to spend my time doing what I do best: speaking!

Where can you find people to help you? I go to elance.com. If you don't know this site, you need to check them out. You can put out a particular job and have people BID for your work. You can get work done cheaply and effectively. I now use them all the time.

When Should You Go Full Time?

Many people start out speaking as a sideline, in addition to their full time job. Not a bad idea, but remember a few key things: you will be able to go out on your own full time as a speaker only if you keep your overhead low.

I would also suggest you have at least six to twelve months' income in your savings or investment account. It may take that amount of time to get your career fully up and running.

One of my early mentors, a man named Howard Shenson told me that the best thing that could ever happen to me would be to get fired. That was back when I was still employed. His point was that when you have no other options, you have to perform.

It will also be much easier for you to go full time if you have created products like I have described in this book. These items will start generating you additional income almost immediately. It will make it easier for you to go out full time if you have a line of products.

To Staff or Not to Staff

There are a lot of speakers who feel their success is based on the number of people they employ. In my opinion, this is ridiculous.

I don't know what your goals are, but mine are to make as much money as possible with the least amount of hassle and aggravation. I can feel a lot of heads nodding as you are reading this right now!

I know highly successful speakers with large staffs and others that are one person shops. I currently operate without an assistant. In the future, if I do have any help, it will be one assistant.

If you like the idea of having a big office with a lot of staff, you better read someone else's book, because I can't help you. I like the idea of keeping things small and manageable, although it would be nice to have a personal assistant.

The bottom-line is that you should be much more concerned with what you NET than what you GROSS.

If you agree with my philosophy on keeping things lean and mean, then let me give you a piece of advice. Don't hire someone with the same skill sets as yourself. Hire someone with complementary skills sets.

If you aren't very organized, look for someone who is, and so forth.

Before you hire any staff, make sure to define what you want that person to do. There should be no surprises for them or you. Have a very specific list of things you will want them to do. Ask them when you interview them about those specific tasks.

If you do hire someone, do it on a trial basis originally. Get them to sign a trial employment contract. Talk to a lawyer when you get to this stage, but it will be a great help if any problems arise in the first couple of months.

I'd also recommend that you check out a site called www.kolbe.com. This can help you hire more effectively.

Working with Your Spouse

If you are working with your spouse and they are your assistant, GOOD LUCK! Some people can pull this off without ending up in divorce court, but it takes an unusual combination of individuals. If you have to start that way, then do it. But as soon as you can, try to hire someone else to replace them. It will be better for both your business and your relationship. Trust me, I've tried it!

Watch Out for Sharks

As in any business, there are certain people who prey on new speakers. If you are just starting, be wary of any and everyone who will offer you a system to turn you into the world's greatest speaker.

Some of the people who pitch you may be legitimate, but most are not. My suggestion is to ask about their guarantee policy. If someone will not give you a complete 100% money back guarantee, I wouldn't deal with them myself. It makes me leery.

Also, before you spend a dime with people, I would recommend that you ask them for the names of five or more of their customers that you can call and speak to before you make a decision regarding their product or service.

Watch how they react when you ask them this question. If they give you the names without a fuss, call them and ask those people some very pointed questions. If you get answers you are happy with, proceed with caution.

Contact me directly if you have any questions on a specific individual. I'll tell you if it's worth spending money with them. My number is 702-617-4206.

Taking the Long Term View

If you are looking to make a quick buck, professional speaking is not for you. Get into some other line of business. The most money and highest profitability for you as a speaker will come after you have established yourself in the marketplace. As you become better known, more people will come to you. As they come to you, you will have to do less outbound marketing. This will lower your costs. As you lower these costs, you will make more money.

Also, as more and more people are put into your database, your mailings will generate more money. Those who buy from you will be much more apt to buy again, further increasing your profitability.

The more you speak, the better you will get. If this isn't the case, there is a big problem. The more you speak, the more people will hear you and refer you to others. The more referrals you generate, the more profitable you will be.

The more you speak, the more those same groups will want you back. If you are only looking at the speaking business as a one-shot deal, with any organization, you are missing the boat. Some highly successful speakers get over 90% of their business from repeat and referral clients. When this is the case for you, your marketing costs will drop to next to nothing. Your profits will increase geometrically.

The moral of the story? Deliver more than what you promised as a speaker and stay in it for the long haul. That's the only way to really make millions as a speaker.

Time Management for Speakers

Go to a Franklin-Covey seminar. This will be your biggest help in learning how to manage your time as a speaker.

I actually leave the office when I want to get something done. I leave the cell phone behind and head to the library or my local Barnes and Noble. I can usually be two or three times more productive.

Find out which times of day you are most productive. Some people can do their best work early in the morning, others late in the evening; don't fight it. Go with what works for you. I have written most of this book in the first few hours after I get up in the morning, the very early hours before business actually gets started.

Remember, as a speaker you need to be writing as well as speaking. Don't put off doing the other things you need to do to be successful. These elements are as important your speaking.

Try to do all of your marketing related activities during normal business hours. It is tough to reach people (if that is what your marketing efforts entail) after business hours. So leave those times reserved for only those activities.

Do all of your other errands at times when you can't be in contact with people to sell yourself and your speaking services.

Other than these few suggestions, I suggest you speak to the true experts on the topic, the people at Franklin-Covey.

Speaking Terminology:
Keynotes, Seminars or Workshops

As a speaker, you need to understand some basic terminology in the industry.

A keynote speech (when the term is properly used) refers to a relatively short speech running from between 30 to 90 minutes. Keynote speakers are usually showmen (and women). They are more motivational than informational.

A keynote is also a one way street. The speaker talks directly to the audience with little or NO interaction.

A seminar is a term used for a more substantive presentation which is usually longer in length than a keynote, usually anywhere from 2 to 6 hours or more in length. The seminar is characterized by a certain degree of interaction between the speaker and participants.

A workshop is similar to a seminar, but much more interactive.

The problem is there is no universal agreement on the terms. These are my rough definition of these terms. You may find others who disagree. You are also apt to find additional terms other than these cropping up all the time.

Trainer or Speaker?

Can a speaker also be a trainer? Absolutely! Are they the same thing? Not at all. A trainer is someone whose primary mission is to transfer information to a group of people effectively. This is very different from a speaker whose primary mission is to entertain. The secondary mission of a speaker is to educate.

If you are more of a performer and a motivator, you are more likely to be a speaker. Speaking is more show business and performance.

Training is more geared to information transfer and is therefore often found in a different type of person than a speaker.

If you are more of a trainer type, does this mean you can't legitimately call yourself a speaker? Not these days. The lines have become blurry.

Keynotes

Keynotes, as I described earlier, are a short form presentation, ranging from 30 – 90 minutes.

The key to your success as a keynote speaker is to do your homework. This should be done before your event through your pre-program questionnaire.

Customization will show your audience that you have done your homework. They will be much more open to your message and to you as a speaker.

How you dress for your keynote will be an issue. I like to look as good as the best dressed person in the audience. I don't like to overdress, however. If everyone in the group is dressed casually, I don't want to have on a suit and tie.

Find this out ahead of time so as not to embarrass yourself or alienate your audience.

The two most important elements of your keynote will be your opening and your closing. You have very little time with your group so you need to grab them immediately. Don't go for a slow build, grab them from the very start. If you want to see how a great opening works, go to your local video store and rent the "The French Connection."

Your opening might be a great story, a shocking statistic or a powerful quotation. Whatever you use, make it something that will make them want to sit up and take notice.

Give them something they'll want to remember and take notes on within the first three minutes of your speech. This will show them you can deliver true value.

Finally, you'll want to close with something memorable and useful.

In the limited time you have, don't try to give your audience more than three key points. Many a keynote speaker makes this mistake. It is deadly. Your outline should be your three points sandwiched between a great opening and a great closing.

If the group you are speaking to has a theme for their meeting, do everything you can to tie that theme into your speech.

Speaking Organizations

There are a number of organizations that are relevant to speakers. Let me give you an overview of each. Before I do that remember not to spend all your time commiserating with your peers. It may be fun, but it seldom generates revenue.

National Speakers Association

Here is an area that my frank talk will get me in hot water. But as you can probably guess, I don't care!

NSA is the only association of professional speakers in the country. It costs around $500 to join.

The stated goal of the association is to advance the cause of professional speakers. I'm sure that the original mission of the organization (from talking to some of the earliest members) was honorable.

I've been a member for a number of years. In the first couple of years of my membership, I found a lot of the information that they gave at their conventions fairly helpful. Soon thereafter, the conventions and events got a little old.

I would hear the same stuff, over and over again. One of the more annoying things is that people took themselves much too seriously. Someone has yet to tell a number of the speakers out there that they aren't movie stars or celebrities. If you go to a convention, you'll see what I mean.

Another area where I had a problem was that quite often the organization proved to be a triumph of **contacts over competence**. Many speakers selected to address the group were neither good speakers nor possessed any good content. BUT, they knew the right people. This is ridiculous. An organization of speakers shouldn't have weak presenters on the platform. This is a travesty.

NSA also has two professional designations which they grant to certain select members. Again, the members who have these designations think they are of vital importance. I have yet to see **any** correlation between these designations and income or competence of the speakers.

It also tends to be a very cliquish group. True of many groups, not just this one.

Here's a couple of specific examples. In 1995 or so I was supposed to address the local chapter of an organization in Northern California. They then disinvited me less than two weeks before the date. Anyone in the speaking business knows this is completely unacceptable behavior.

The group has a very hard time dealing with people like me. The "in your face" individual who has a lot to offer but won't put up with the BS that organizations like this tend to be filled with.

Why am I still there? Because I believe that the best way to TRY to change an organization is from within. It will be interesting to see what happens as I become even more successful.

I have a number of good friends who are members, but the group as a whole is hard for me to take.

So what's my suggestion? Join it for a year. Go to a convention or two. See if it works for you. After that point, if you like the camaraderie, continue to go. If not, do what I do. Keep your membership intact, but don't waste your time or money on the conventions. I don't mean to be cynical, but I am speaking the truth. I have a hard time doing it any other way.

Local Chapters of NSA

There are also local chapters of the NSA. These vary dramatically around the country. Some are very active and helpful and some are not. Early on in your speaking career I suggest you attend some of your local events as well. Remember that these chapters are often run by some very power-hungry individuals who have egos the size of a small planet.

A former friend of mine now doesn't even return my phone calls in one chapter. Why? I have no idea, but it gives you the idea of the politics that are involved here.

Toastmasters

Toastmasters is a training organization for new speakers. If you are just starting out, it may be worth looking for a chapter near you. They have a specific curriculum for you to go through if you're just starting out. Check the resource section for their number and address. I mentioned them earlier. They can be reached at www.toastmasters.org.

ASTD

The American Society of Training and Development is an organization geared to those who do training. This organization is worth looking into. Contact them and find out if they have a local chapter in your city. If they do, go to a meeting.

IPA

You may also hear about a group called the International Platform Association. I cannot recommend them. I went to one of their meetings once and found it completely useless.

Public Seminar Companies

Public seminar companies are those large organizations that send out massive numbers of brochures promoting every seminar topic you could possibly imagine.

If you aren't on their lists, get on them. The public seminar companies would include Dunn and Bradstreet, Padgett Thompson, SkillPath and The Covey Institute. Watch what they are promoting. This will give you a good idea of which topics are hot. They are very rarely innovators, but they are very good followers. Watch what they do and learn. They aren't in business to lose money.

For four years I worked with one of the biggest ones in the world: CareerTrack. Now defunct.

It was a very interesting experience. If people ask if me if I'd do it again, on balance I'd have to say no. There are pluses and minuses in working with a public seminar; you can decide for yourself.

Positives

First, the positives. You get an awful lot of experience doing these gigs. For four years I spent 100 or more days doing primarily full-day seminars. This is incredibly great experience, but it's also tremendously exhausting.

You will also get plenty of practice doing product sales. Even though the products are not your own, this experience is invaluable to you.

FREE SPEAKING TIPS:

To receive regular tips on how to start and build a successful speaking business send an email to:

tips@professionalspeakingsuccess.com.

Negatives

You should know that most professional speakers look down their noses at people who work with these public seminar companies. You are looked at as if you couldn't quite make the big leagues when you work with them.

The problem with working with them is that you tend to get stuck working with them. You make enough money so that some people have a tendency to get lazy. If you want to make really big money you should be using this experience as a stepping stone, not as the end all and be all.

The routine involves driving from city to city each day. You usually have to drive at least two hours, get up the next morning and do another full day seminar. Most weeks you have to work at least 4 days. This is tremendously exhausting.

Money

You can expect to get paid somewhere in the $500 a day range. What this will do is keep you at the subsistence level as a speaker. You will be able to tell your friends and family that you speak professionally, but you won't be making any serious money.

What to Say to People When They Ask What You Do

You will get asked the question in a variety of different circumstances: What do you do?

You should have a very well prepared answer to this question in two or three lengths. The first one you should have is what is often called your "elevator" pitch. This is a one sentence description of what you do. It should be sufficiently intriguing for people to want to hear more.

You might also have different pitches depending on the circumstances under which you meet a person. Your answer at the local rotary club meeting might be different than if you are at a trade show of chemical engineers.

My most common elevator pitch is this: "I help small to medium sized businesses double or triple their sales in 18 months or less or I don't get paid." After I deliver this line, the most common response is: "Really? How do you do that?" That response allows me to get going on delivering the rest of my pitch - the more detailed 30 second pitch.

I would then continue: "I work with a variety of businesses to help them dramatically increase their sales through the use of some very specific proprietary marketing techniques that I have developed. These are techniques that have been proven to work in a variety of industries. When I work with a company the bulk of my compensation is contingent upon generating results. If I don't deliver, I don't get paid."

You need to develop one of each of these "blurbs" as a minimum. I have a number of different ones developed for each of my targeted niche markets.

Marketing Your Speaking Business

Your Speaking Promotional Material

I want to discuss the basic promotional materials that every speaker must have. I have worked with a lot of speakers to help them develop their speaking materials and I know what you need to have and what works best.

They include:

- Your book
- Testimonial letters
- Tiered brochure
- Audio demo tapes
- Web site
- Business cards
- One-page, faxable brochure
- Free giveaway items
- Video demo tapes
- Postcards

Let's cover each of these items in order.

Many speakers spend entirely too much time and money on their promotional materials. Your most important promotional materials are your book and your letters of recommendation. Let me repeat: your BOOK and your LETTERS OF RECOMMENDATION. The book won't cost you that much per unit, and the testimonials are dirt cheap to duplicate.

Do not spend big money on fancy four color brochures. It will be a dramatic waste of your money. After you are a nationally known speaker, then you will have to have super expensive promotional material to justify the huge fees they are paying you.

You can pray for that problem.

Your Book

This item is discussed in detail on page 52. I also have written a book and done an entire seminar on this topic. For more information go to www.selfpublishingsuccess.com.

Business Cards

As far as business cards go, it is a good idea to keep them simple. Having a picture on them won't hurt. Make sure and call yourself a "speaker/consultant/author." Put all of your important information on the card including your email address and web site.

One Page Faxable Sheet

You need to have a one page summary of your speaking business. This one page should give anyone who is interested a general overview of you and your business. You should include a brief bio, a short list of clients, the topics you speak on, a few powerful testimonials, your picture and your contact information. Give whomever you send it to enough to make them want to know more.

Letters of Recommendation

Letters of recommendation are one your most powerful tools in getting speaking engagements. Here's a story to illustrate.

A speaker was asked by a potential client to send them some information. Rather than putting some fancy four color brochure and a video in a well designed "speaker package", he sends out 50 - 60 letters of recommendation in a box wrapped with duct tape. The speaker got the business.

Nothing is more powerful than other people putting on paper how good you were when you spoke to their group.

I actually put a referral clause in my contract. This requires them to give me a great testimonial if they are happy.

The 2 keys to getting great letters of recommendation are to do a great job on the platform AND to get them to write them while they're hot. Immediately after the presentation people still have you fresh in their minds. They remember how great you were. If you wait, they tend to forget how well you did.

Keep the original letters of recommendation well protected. They are worth their weight in gold.

As you get more and more letters, separate them into categories. When you have plenty of them in the file cabinet, send out only those that are from the industry where you are courting someone.

Tiered Brochure/Folder

Your presentation folder is what will hold the elements of your tiered brochure. You can look for presentation folders. You can buy the inexpensive, generic ones at Office Max or Staples. When you get further along in your career, you may want to get them customized with your name on the outside. When you're first getting started, keep them simple and keep them cheap.

I use the term "tiered" brochure because on the right hand side of the folder you put four sheets of paper, each one slightly larger than the other sheet behind it, creating a tiered effect.

The shortest element in the tiered brochure would be your bio. Make it the shortest element so people don't think you are too full of your-self. Elements of the bio can be put into bullet or paragraph form. Give them the highlights of your life. Don't go too far back. There is no need to include your winning record as a third-grade speller.

The next largest sheet would be your list of clients. If you have limit-ed clients, write a paragraph description for each of them. If there are plenty of clients to list, list them in multiple columns on the page. If you have tons of clients to list, you may want to divide them by industry category as well.

The next largest sheet on the right hand side of the page would be your list of program offerings. Take your three or four topics that you speak on and put them on one page using one full paragraph to describe each one of them.

Your largest sheet of paper, which sits at the back of all the other sheets, is an individual, full page description of each of your topics. This is the chance for you to give a full and complete description of each of your topics.

Give Away Items

You need to have something to give away for free that has value and demonstrates your brilliant speaking skills and content. It should be in a number of different forms. You'll need to have this audio in cassette form as well as CD.

If the item is promoting you and your business, I always put a line on the outside of the tape that says it can be duplicated. It's sort of the opposite of what most people might think to do. As far as I'm concerned, I'd like to get as many copies of these tapes out there to help my speaking career.

Leave copies of your cassette or CD in places where people might find them, pick them up and listen to them. I would recommend that you do this with your video materials, but with current technology, it is too expensive to do so.

Before you start leaving these items in grocery stores, think about what the demographics are of the places you start leaving these things lying around. My preferred location to leave these are in airline clubs at the airport and on airplanes.

If you have this material out there for people to find, make sure to make it easy for them to find you. Your toll free number should be all over the cassette or CD.

Have a bounceback offer imbedded in the audio. Make sure to give people some kind of great offer if they will contact you as a result of hearing your audio. My preferred example is to offer people a critique of someone's current marketing materials. This gives me the opportunity to get back to them with some great suggestions and give them a sample of my marketing brilliance. They are also in my database permanently as well.

Audio Demo Tape

The demo audio tape used to be the primary method speakers had of marketing themselves. Given that everyone and his brother now owns a VCR, it is imperative to have a demo video.

If you are just starting out, however, the demo audio is an inexpensive way for you to let people know what your speaking skills are like.

You can make this tape as lengthy as you want as long as it's interesting. The first few minutes of your audio demo tape should give highlights and snippets from some of your more engaging and interesting programs.

You can then follow this section with a more in-depth and complete audio program for people to listen to.

Video Demo Tape

Other than great testimonials, your demo video tape is the most important element of your promotional material as a speaker.

If people are looking to hire you as a speaker, they want to see you speak. The demo tape is how you prove to people that see your demo that you are a good speaker and worthy of being hired.

Your demo tape must be made in such a way to get your prospects attention instantly. Remember, those who are reviewing the tapes might be looking at twenty or thirty of these tapes. You must first catch their attention at the beginning of your video to make sure they stay to see the rest of it. It is very much like what a good author must do in the beginning of their books.

The demo tape shouldn't be longer than six to eight minutes. I would then suggest you attach a much longer, more in-depth presentation onto the end of the video. Many meeting planners want to see a long unedited section of tape and material.

I have two different demo videos, one that is bureau friendly and one that is for my own direct contacts and potential clients. Don't confuse the two. Send the bureaus the demos with none of your contact information on the video.

Many speakers sit down in a video editing suite and get completely carried away. I know a lot about videos and video creation, more than any speaker I know. I have produced hundreds of how to videos. The one thing I don't do on any video is to make the effects the star.

Don't make the mistake of making your video so filled with video pizzazz that people miss the content and style that you are trying to communicate.

Try to get all of your presentations video taped. I videotape the majority of my presentations on a digital video system. If I am going to be doing a big "gig" I will try to get a camera crew that has professional equipment to capture the event. I then use this footage in my video tape.

Remember that you can't get a good end product (your finished demo) without good original footage. Don't use a poor camera and expect that you will be able to create a good looking final demo. It just won't happen.

Many times I will let my clients video tape my presentations and use the information in exchange for the masters. I can then cut them together as I see fit for demo purposes.

The worst offense for your video demo is to be boring. You can make it anything else, but don't make it boring.

Websites

Every speaker needs to have a web site. This site should be a showcase for you, your products and your speaking ability. I would suggest simple rather than busy and/or fancy. It would be best for you to take your name and get it registered with the "dot com" attached to it.

Remember your goal for your speaking website. It is to get people, once they go to your site, to either request more information or book you as a speaker. The other option is that you might be able to get people to buy product from your web site. In the event that people buy your products, they might later come to you to ask you to speak to their group or company.

Your website as a speaker should have a place where people can click and see a sample video of your presentation skills.

Postcards

I think every speaker should have a collection of postcards that are unique to you and your organization to keep in touch with people who are either prospects or existing customers.

A handwritten postcard is ten times more effective than a typewritten letter or email. You can also use postcards to promote events by sending people to a specific website where you close with a longer sales letter.

The Future for Speaking Promo Materials

As internet technology improves, speakers will eventually be able to have both audio and video clips available for prospects to look at on the web. They will be immediately downloadable. It will be great when this happens because there will be a huge cost savings for speakers on promotional materials. You will no longer have to have demo tapes or printed promotional materials. People will go to the web and download what they want to see.

Getting Pictures of Yourself

You need to get some professional pictures taken of yourself. Pay for a qualified professional to take some great shots. There is nothing worse than a bad picture. Those would include hands near your face and other old and trite techniques.

Most of the time you will simply need a black and white headshot. But if you do pay for a photo session, make sure to get some color shots as well. Get both casual and more business-oriented shots.

Get some "action" shots, those where you are shown in the act of speaking. Also, get any picture you can with celebrities.

Both your clients and the media will ask you for pictures. Make sure and have a recent one available. Not long ago I saw a picture of a speaker who in person looked 25 years older. This is misrepresentation. Don't do it. Make yourself look good, but not THAT good.

Setting Your Fees

I'm sure you're excited to hear about how much money you can make as a speaker. I don't blame you; it's one of the reasons I got into the business! So here is some very important information on fees and fee setting.

Speaking fees have got to be divided into three categories. Beginning speaker fees, "Regular" speaking fees, and Celebrity speaking fees. Beginning speakers must charge enough to be considered credible. When you first start out, charge less than these minimal amounts and frankly you'll be perceived as a joke. No one who has any knowledge of speaking fees will think you are worth a damn if you ask for less than $500, regardless of how long you're going to be speaking.

Another "dirty little secret" of the speaking business is that speakers lie about their fees and incomes. I guess they want to sound like they're making more than they really are. When I first started going to speaking conventions the not-so-unspoken rule was to divide everything everyone said by at least two. Many speakers were exaggerating the truth.

If you are uncomfortable charging the numbers I will list here, then you need to work on improving your message and delivery. In most cases, the concern about charging fees that you deserve is a mental hang-up on your part.

The first thing to remember as a professional speaker is that unless you set your fees at certain minimal levels, people will not take you seriously.

The one thing you will always hear speakers say is that they don't negotiate their fees. They are either lying or they're stupid. There are certain times when you should negotiate fees. You should have set fees and then offer very credible discounts based on certain factors.

You will not be perceived as credible if you don't charge certain minimum numbers. Celebrity speakers are making upwards of $50,000 a speech. A celebrity speaker would be someone like Christopher Reeve, Norman Schwarzkopf, or Anthony Robbins. Celebrity speakers are almost always best selling authors and people who have had high visibility in the public eye for a long time.

Numbers like this are not in your immediate picture, unless you are a celebrity as I described. If you are and you're reading this book, please pick it up and take it to the counter and buy it. You can afford it!

With the plan that I'm giving you here you may not end up with celebrity speaking fees, but you can certainly progress to the upper tier level of speakers.

Non-celebrity speakers are in a caste system (of a sort) based on fees. The top non celebrity speaker will charge somewhere between $10,000 – $15,000 per keynote speech. Very few people fall into this category. No more than 1 or 2% of speakers fall into this category.

You need to come up with a few different fees that everyone will ask you about. The main ones are your keynote, 1/2 day and full day fee.

Adjust your fees upward as you start to get more work. The amount of work you are getting when charging a given rate is the only indication of whether or not your fees are set correctly. And remember, if your fees are set at a certain level and you aren't getting any bites, you are obviously priced too high for the market.

My fees are set at the following rates: $4,500 for a keynote, $5,500 for a half day and $6,500 for a full day. This is a good rule of thumb in terms of the ratios between the different length programs.

If you charge "x" for your keynote, you need to charge "x" times 1.2 or 1.25 to arrive at your half-day rate. To get your full day rate, take your keynote rate and multiply it by 1.5 – 1.75. Again these are just guidelines. Once you start speaking you will get the hang of the fee setting exercise.

A beginning speaker should start by charging no less than $750 for a keynote. This is a rate that you should charge before you start pursuing the Speakers Bureaus. They will want you to charge at least $2,000 for any length of presentation in order to represent you. This, for the obvious reason that they can do just as much work (and possibly less) and get twice the fee that they would from you with a speaker who is charging $4,000 or $5,000.

When you work with Bureaus, they like to know that the fees you charge are consistent. They want to know that your fees haven't been "jacked up" because of the fact that you will have to pay them a commission.

Keep your fee schedule consistent. This will make it so you don't alienate the Bureaus. If you work with them a lot, this is important.

What to do When They Call and You're Already Booked

Let's hope that the biggest problem you have as a speaker is having to turn away people when they call you because you're already booked to speak elsewhere on the same date.

Rather than turn this business away, try to find a way to turn it into money for you. Even if you can't do a particular date, have a couple of other speakers who you can refer clients to.

Have an arrangement set up where you will receive 10% (a lot lower than what a bureau charges) for passing along the speaking date to them.

If it is someone with whom you refer dates back and forth to each other on a regular basis, it may not make sense to send each of them your 10% referral fees.

The key is not to just say no, but to try to generate revenue even from dates that you can't do.

Speaker Negotiation Techniques

Never say "yes" to a date immediately. You will appear like you're not in demand. When someone calls in, ask a lot of questions first before you quote a price. When you do give out a price, put the quote in terms of a range.

Then ask them a series of questions. Here are a few.

- Who did you use last year?

- What is the budget?

- How many people will be attending?

- What is the purpose of the convention?

- How long did you want me to speak?

- Is there a special program for the managers and directors?

- How would you like to use my handouts and promo materials?

Only after you have gotten these key questions answered should you give out a price. If you give your price and hear them sigh on the other end of the phone, you know your number is higher than they expected. Either that or they are great negotiators.

You then have a choice. Do you really want to speak to this group? Is there a possibility for big product sales numbers? Is speaking to this organization going to give you other non-financial benefits?

If you decide you want to lower your price, find a way to cut the price without making it seem like you really are. If the group you want to speak for has a newsletter, you may want to ask them for free advertising space in addition to a reduced rate on your normal speaking fee.

It may actually make you more money to take them up on this arrangement. Don't dismiss this strategy. Consider it an option.

Record Everything You Do

I have been guilty of not doing what I am about to tell you to do.

So, as the old saying goes, "do as I say, not as I do." Record everything you do. It would be preferable to get it on video, but recording everything on audio would be a minimum.

There are three main reasons for recording your presentations.

First, you may catch a "magic moment" on tape. The biggest disappointment every speaker has is to do something really great and then not have a record of it. If you do have everything on tape and a magic moment occurs, you can use it in your next batch of promotional material.

The second reason you want to tape everything is to make sure you have a record of your product presentation. If you are doing as I suggest, product sales will soon become a very significant portion of your income. Don't forget to listen to each of your product presentations to see how you did.

Every once in a while you will sell a boatload of products. Most speakers have no earthly idea why it worked so well on that particular occasion. With a tape of the event, you will have a better chance of figuring it out.

The third reason is you may be able to turn a certain number of those recordings into products. I do! And they have made me over a million dollars in the last few years. Recording an event live and selling it as a product requires no editing. If recorded properly (so you can hear audience questions), there is no better product that you can create.

Why would you want to record something if you already had it? First, some people will be willing to buy these tapes even if they have a recording of basically the same event already. Why? They are interested in the questions from the audience, which are always different.

They also think that they may pick up something different. Perhaps they will, maybe not in substance, but in style. Why disappoint them? They are willing to pay for this information, so give it to them.

Another good reason is this. If for some reason you sell twice as many products from the platform one day, you want to know why. You will not know why unless you go back and carefully examine your pitch.

You may also catch that elusive magic moment in your presentation. If you don't record an event, that may be the event where the magic happens.

If you don't record the whole event, at least record your product pitch. This is critical. After all, product sales will account for a substantial portion of your revenue base.

Cultivating Your Database

Your most important asset as a speaker is your database of names that you acquire from the speeches you give. To repeat, your database is your MOST important asset as a speaker.

This means that you must first make sure to acquire the names of those for whom you speak.

This also means that you must try to convince the meeting planner, or whomever your contact is, to give you the list of people who will be attending the event in which you will be speaking. This will sometimes be difficult.

Try to sell the person on how important it is for you to keep in touch with those who hear you speak for greater effectiveness. Although this is true, it is also the best sales pitch you can use to get the names.

If you can't get them that way, ask people to put each of their business cards in a hat for a drawing for something of value at some point during your presentation.

As soon as you get back to your office, put their emails into your database as soon as possible. The longer you wait, the less apt it is to get done.

What database? I use a program called webmarketingmagic. For anyone who has not yet bought anything from me, the only thing I want from them is their email address. Webmarketingmagic can handle hundreds of thousands of email addresses, or, as little as a few hundred.

After someone buys something from me, I move them into my database in ACT! When they become a buyer, I now want all of their contact information. Before they buy, emails alone will do.

I use ACT, but any database will do. I would prefer you use a contact management program over a database. The difference lies in the fact that a contact management program is more conducive to making and keeping notes about each person in your database.

When the event is over, make sure you mail an offer to the participants immediately after the event. Target those who didn't buy from you at the event. They will be most likely to buy from you soon after they have seen you, if ever.

The average value of each person in my database is well over $100. I treat my database like gold!

Handling Inquiries

A speaker's office should be set up to accomplish one primary goal. The goal is to generate the maximum amount of income through maximizing the number of speaking engagements and product sales.

To accomplish this, you need to have things systematized. When you have systems, things will get done quickly and efficiently. Creating systems will also mean that fewer things will fall through the cracks.

The first system that needs to be set up is on how to handle an inquiry.

At my office, when someone calls the first thing I do is fill out a lead sheet. You can easily prepare one of your own. Make sure it includes all of the standard pertinent information like name, phone number, date of the event, email address, etc. This sheet makes certain that you ask all the right questions so as not to forget anything that you should have asked.

Even 15 years after getting started as a speaker, I still use a lead sheet. It makes it so I never forget to ask the critical questions. You should follow my lead on this one.

Some people prefer to skip the hard copy "inquiry sheet" and enter the data directly into their computer database. I don't recommend this. Even though it seems like I am recommending you do double work, I still recommend the inquiry sheet.

First, you can usually write faster than you can type. Second, it will sound better to the caller. They won't hear the keyboard keys ticking away as you enter their information and data. If and when they do hear the keyboard, I think it makes them feel much more like a number and less like an individual who deserves your full attention.

Lastly, you have hard copy back up. If you keep the inquiry sheets, enter the information at the end of the day and then file them by date. After you enter the information from the inquiry sheet into the computer you have to decide what action you will take.

If you send out all of your expensive promotional material to everyone who called, you would go broke. You first have to assess whether the lead you get is a high, medium, or low probability lead. Remember, a lead may start as a low probability lead and work its way up the ladder.

For a low probability lead, my office will fax them a one page sheet, email them a standard email and direct them to my web site. For a medium probability lead the office will send out a video demo tape and press kit via USPS priority mail. For a high probability lead we will do the same as the medium lead, but send it via Federal Express.

How do you determine what level of lead has come in? Practice. When you first get started you will think everything is high probability. Trust me, it's not. Don't waste a lot of money on sending out expensive promo material unless you are certain they are close to making a decision.

If a call comes in and gets picked up by a machine, make sure you get back to people in a timely fashion or risk losing a job.

Speaker Tracking Form

In addition to doing a great job on the platform, your success as a speaker will be judged by how well you handle the administrative elements of the business. Like it or not, this is true.

Once you get a signed contract, you need to make sure that everything goes smoothly all the way through your speaking date and even after the engagement is done.

Take a look at the checklist at the back of this book. This is a good place to start. As you kick your speaking business into full gear, you will make your own changes. That's fine, but this is a good place to start. The checklist will make it so that you don't miss anything crucial that you are supposed to do.

This way you can go down the sheet and check off the tasks as they are completed. If you don't do this you risk forgetting one or more very important items. When you screw up with a client in this way you will look very unprofessional. Your chance of future bookings will be dramatically reduced.

When you get a serious lead for a speaking engagement, create a temporary file. In addition to any correspondence you have with the prospect, you should also put your checklist in the front of the file.

Once that person signs the contract, you will create a permanent file and then transfer all the elements from the temporary file to the permanent file. This will include the very important checklist.

Periodically pull out the sheet and see what you have and haven't done. It will help you not to miss anything important.

Ways to Make Money as a Speaker

You can make money as a speaker in a variety of ways.

You can generate your own speaking engagements going directly to organizations and speaking in-house, doing presentations to corporations and associations. You can also do these same in-house presentations where you are booked by a speakers bureau.

You can also do an open to the public event. There are two primary ways of doing this. One way is to have another entity promote you and your seminar, the other is where you promote and publicize the event yourself.

When you promote yourself in an "open to the public" forum. You do all of the work. You place and pay for the advertising. You do all of the work, but you make all of the money. That assumes that you make money. If you want more information on promoting your own seminars, you may want to check out the website: www.seminarexpert.com. Better yet, send an email to: tips@seminarexpert.com and get a course that usually costs $77, yours free because you read it here.

You can also make money from the sales of your products. This includes any and everything you offer for sale at your speaking events. Many successful speakers make as much as 50% or more of their income from the sales of various forms of products.

You'll also be called on to do consulting work. For more information on this topic, take a look at my site: www.consultingexpert.com.

Start with a Market, Not with a Topic

A great way to decide where to go with your speaking career is to find a market you know something about and figure out what information they need to hear.

This system will make your speaking business more "market driven." If you have a great seminar or speech and no one is interested in the topic, then you're in big trouble.

Take a look at the fields where you have expertise and ask yourself what you can offer these groups that they would pay for. Find this out by polling the groups. They will generally give you some interesting answers.

Selecting a Topic

So you want to be a speaker but you don't know what you want to talk about. This is a problem.

The most important point to remember when selecting a topic is to choose something you love to learn about. I love marketing. So that is what I speak about.

Make sure that you don't select a topic strictly based on what's hot at any given moment.

I remember meeting an aspiring speaker at an event. He told me he wanted to be a speaker. I asked him what his topic was. He said he didn't have one, but he could speak on anything. This is MAJOR problem.

Someone who can speak on anything will be a weak speaker. Clearly, the degree of passion for whatever topic he/she comes up with will be questionable.

Also, be careful of labeling yourself as a "motivational" speaker. It's great that you can speak in a highly motivational fashion, but few will pay for these types of speakers. You need more than just motivation in any speech. The only speakers who get work as motivational speakers are former Olympic athletes, current athletes and a few others.

Speak about what gets you excited. It will be much easier that way.

Niche Marketing: Your Key to Speaking Success

Let me give you an example to illustrate a point. Years ago, I got booked to speak for the Self Storage Association. They paid me $5,000 for a one hour keynote.

Over the past five years, I have developed an extensive line of audio and video products for this market. I have also written the only book on self-storage marketing.

I now promote a lot of my own speaking events to this particular industry. Many of them are very high priced events like bootcamps. I do an average of 15 – 20 days a year of lucrative one-on-one consulting work with people in this same industry.

Why do I tell you this story? Because it's easier to be a big fish in a little pond. But that doesn't mean you only have to pick one pond to swim in. If you want to have little or no competition in the speaking business, carve out a niche and start doing everything you possibly can to become KING/QUEEN of that market niche.

That would include:

- Writing articles for their trade publications
- Writing a book targeted at that individual niche
- Speaking at their trade shows
- Promoting your own seminars and workshops
- Creating and distributing a newsletter specifically geared to the niche
- Creating and promoting a web site for that niche
- Generating publicity for yourself within the niche

Most speakers try to promote themselves to the world at large. This is much too big a target to hit. Granted, if you have a book on the New York Times best seller list, you may be able to make it as a generalist, but for the rest of us mere mortals, the chances are slim.

How do you select your niches?

Two ways. One is to go out and purposely select one, either because you have previous knowledge about the industry or that you have an intense interest in the industry and are willing to immerse yourself in it. The other way is to have the niche thrust upon you.

Let's say you have been working with a speakers bureau and they have booked you to speak at the annual convention of Pest Control owners. You speak and are very warmly received by the group. Why not use this as your launching pad for attacking this individual market. After all, you already have been conveniently introduced.

After you've read this book, you will have developed products specific to this niche before you even get to the event.

If this were to happen, you have to strike quickly. They will forget about you if you wait too long. Do everything I suggest in this book (on the marketing side) as quickly as possible. This will give you your greatest chance for success.

The Key to Marketing as a Speaker

No one likes to beg for anything. Nor does any speaker want to beg to be selected to speak at someone's event. The key is to get people to call you. Either that, or sponsoring your own events which puts you in the driver's seat.

Your whole marketing emphasis should be geared to getting your phone to ring from people who want you to speak. There are two ways to do this. One is through "direct" marketing. The other is through "indirect" marketing. The only direct marketing that you should be doing is to promote your own events.

By indirect marketing I mean anything and everything you do (book and article writing, etc.) that will get people to call you up and get them into your funnel.

Forming Your Association(s)

It may be a good idea to start your own association. This will give you the designation of "president" of XYZ association. This tactic is particularly effective if you are targeting a niche market. In my case, one of my markets is video producers. Making myself the president of the "Video Producers Marketing Association" makes it easier for me to get booked as a speaker in that industry.

Don't spend a lot of money to set up the association, but it will help your credibility. An association doesn't have to be set up as a non-profit. Starting an association will give you both added clout and visibility. It will be easier for you to get media coverage.

Starting an association and becoming president of that association makes you the king of the hill. This will be helpful to your speaking success because you will be in a high visibility position.

Researching Your Topic

In order to be an effective speaker, you have to know your topic inside out. There are a number of ways to do this.

The first place to go is to the web. Put in the key words that relate to your topic, and you will get a lot of information. The problem will be sorting through the information. For that, you're on your own.

The next place for you to go is to the library. Talk to and befriend your reference librarians. They can be very helpful to you, both now and in the future. Look through the periodicals and the books. Use the library computer to search your topic.

My favorite way to research any topic is to interview experts in the field. It's both fun and gives you a lot of great information. You can also make yourself some money if you can get them to agree to have the conversation recorded. Check the section on products to explain this one.

You'll also want to get a hold of any of the major magazines in your field. This will keep you abreast of the specific issues in any of your niche markets.

I also keep CNN on while I am writing. This allows me to incorporate any recent news events in my speeches and seminars. That, in addition to reading the local paper wherever I am as well as USA Today, keeps me up to date on current events.

I got an idea from Lou Heckler (a fellow speaker) on how to use the local paper in any city you are speaking which I think is brilliant. He suggests that you get up early in the morning and scan the local paper where you will be speaking to find a local story that will allow you to further illuminate one or more of your content points in your speech or seminar.

By going through the paper, you will in most cases be able to find a story that almost exactly illustrates a major content point. Take that page of the paper and go down to the front desk of your hotel. Ask them to take that page of the paper and make a copy of it onto a sheet of mylar (that you will provide them). This is a sheet of plain overhead plastic that you can pick up at any office supply store. The copy can be made using this sheet and any standard copy machine.

During your presentation you can pop that overhead up on the screen at the appropriate time to illustrate your point. Your participants and your hosts will be impressed. It is not only good research; it shows you do your homework every day.

There is also a variety of what are called clipping services available. These are companies that will, for a fee, scan the magazines and other media of the world and flag any stories that have certain key words that you provide them with. This tends to be an expensive service. Depending on how far along you are in your speaking career, this may or may not be worth it.

I also like the idea of using the interview as a research tool. Most famous people in a field tend to be media hounds. Take advantage of this fact to get them to give you their time over the phone for an interview. This tool is incredibly effective to get very specific questions answered. Your audience will also be impressed when you can say to them: "In a recent interview I had with John Doe ... "

To get these folks to let you interview them, just locate their phone number and call them. Some will be more than willing to talk to you. Others will not. Expect that and roll with the punches.

Surveys are another great way to get some primary research. Audience members love to hear survey results. Do surveys on issues that are interesting to you and that you yourself want answers to. Remember, no one said that every survey must be done according to the rules set out by the major polling companies.

When I have an issue I want answers to I create a simple survey form on one page and hand it out to anyone, anywhere who will take 3 minutes to fill it out. Many times I will use audiences to fill out a survey and then report those results to them and to others. I suggest you do the same.

When you have a topic that you are excited about, accumulate as much information as you possibly can. Don't worry about where you're going to use it for now, just get as much information as you possibly can. You will find a place for all of it at some point.

When you get up in front of a group to speak and have research to back up what you're saying, you can be a lot more forceful in your presentation. Any topic that you speak on you should be doing some primary research. Don't think that you have to hire the Gallup organization to do some Ph.D. sanctioned research. Most people don't know the different between research done the right way and research done the other way.

Create a simple one-page questionnaire on the topic that you want to research. Hand it to everyone that you meet. No one says that you have to have an absolute random sample.

I have given you an example in this book of some my own primary research. I got close to 1500 people to answer my survey questions on what makes a great speaker. This kind of research worked for this topic, because it was a simple question and I was only asking for one of three answers.

If you have anything more complex that you will need to get the answers to, prepare a very simple survey form that even a fifth grader can answer. This is your best way to go, because you will get the greatest number of responses.

Writing Your Book

One of my bigger mistakes I made as a speaker was not to write a book early on. Don't you do the same. I don't care how hard you think it is or how painful it is for you. YOU MUST WRITE A BOOK! If you are just starting your speaking career, take note. If you are a veteran, you know exactly what I mean.

Why write a book? There are three primary reasons.

First are the fees that you will receive. If you were to take a survey of the fees paid to speakers who are authors and compare those fees to those who aren't, you would find that published authors make substantially more money. The disparity is large and significant. Those who have books make more money. No question!

Second, your access to publicity will be significantly enhanced. You will be able to get on radio and TV a lot easier if you have a book. Net result? You will get more calls as a result of being seen in the media. It is your best ticket to getting speaking engagements.

Third, your book becomes your single best piece of promotional material. The best example I can give you is one that I tell every time I give a speech to a group of speakers. I remember sitting next to a guy on an airplane. We got to talking. After I told him that I was a speaker and consultant, he asked me for a business card. I told him I didn't have a business card on me, but asked if he wanted a copy of my book.

The look on his face was priceless. He was awestruck. People revere authors. Giving someone a copy of your book is the best promotional piece you can use to promote yourself.

Now don't get me wrong; you don't want to be giving out books to people who aren't qualified prospects. But you NEVER want to forget to put a book into the hands of someone who IS.

When an organization or association is looking to book a speaker, it is a much safer choice for them to go with an author. If there is a problem, the person who recommended you can always cover their rear ends by saying that "the guy had a book."

The meeting planner has a much easier time getting you a speaking gig with their company if they can tell the "board", or whomever makes a decision, that you are the author of a book.

If writing a book interests you, go to my website www.selfpublishingsuccess.com. This site will show you exactly how to do your own book. I also have a book called Publishing for Maximum Profit. Call the office to get a copy of it.

First, let me let you in on a little secret. It does not take a genius to write a book. It takes tenacity and perseverance. Moreover, writing a non-fiction book is simple. Simple, but not easy. Keep reading.

There are four steps. First you need to decide on a topic. Pick one that you will both enjoy writing and speaking about. Make sure that there will be demand in the marketplace for your topic. Find out if others are speaking on the topic. If they aren't, BE WORRIED.

Then you have to research the book. Accumulate any and all material you can find: books, magazines, newsletters, on-line research, personal interviews.

Next you have to create an extensive outline of your topic. Put together a minimum of 25 major topic headings which will serve as your chapters. Then gather at least four subtopics to put under each of your chapter headings.

This will give you a total of 100 "units" of information. Write two pages on each and you'll have a 200 page book. If you write just three pages each day you will have the book done in just over two months.

Sound too easy? It is. The main reason why people don't write books is not because of lack of talent or ability. It's because of a lack of perseverance. That in addition to perfectionism. Get over it. Your book will never be perfect.

Your next decision will be to decide if you want to get a publisher to do your book, or if you want to do it on your own. My suggestion is to self-publish. You shouldn't be surprised from the name of my upcoming book, "Publishing for Maximum Profit."

You have 3 choices when it comes to publishing your book. You can use a traditional publisher, use a vanity publisher, or self publish.

Traditional publishers are the New York based publishing companies like Random House, Doubleday and John Wiley. Good luck at even getting these people to even read your book. To get seen by these folks, you most likely will need an agent. I've got a great one for you: Jeffrey Herman. You can reach Jeff at Jeff@jeffherman.com.

I went to Jeff only AFTER I had self-published a number of books on my own. He told me that his job as an agent is much easier. Publishing companies are pretty conservative. They will be much more apt to take on an author who has a track record of writing, printing and selling books.

If you ever get a deal from a traditional publisher it will be a great one from them and a very poor one for you in almost every case. Naturally, they are betting on an unknown and untested entity —

YOU!

Your second option is what is called a "vanity publisher." These are the folks you see advertising in the book review section of any newspaper. The typical ad says: "Manuscripts Wanted." Beware. Accept this deal and you get royally hosed. They will charge you a lot of money and give you very little in exchange. They are the worst of all possible worlds. Avoid them like the plague.

Your third option is self publishing. This is where you do it all yourself. You write it, you print it and you sell it. After you self publish your first or second book you may want to consider going to a traditional publisher.

If you want more information in the area of putting together your book, check the resource section in the back for more information about other products that I have that may be useful to you.

Book Anthologies

You will occasionally get solicited by various groups or individuals to participate in an anthology. This is where someone serves as the organizer and gets a collection of other people to contribute to a book that has chapters done by each of the contributing speakers.

Don't do it. It isn't worth it. I would rather see you dealing other peoples products that you like until you get some of your own, but never an anthology. They look cheesy and you don't make much money.

You need to have products as soon as you can, but this is not the route to go. If you get called for one of these, politely say: "NO THANKS."

Writing for Publications

Writing for publications will be helpful to you in a number of ways.

First, once you have written the articles, you will be able to make copies of them and include them in your "press kit" that you send to anyone who expresses an interest in using you as a speaker. This will increase your credibility. Anyone who has articles published presumably knows what they are talking about. This assumption, by the way, is often incorrect. But this isn't your problem!

Second, you will be getting free exposure to the marketplace. Hopefully the publication will allow you to put in contact information so people can get back in touch with you and leave you their addresses, phone numbers and other relevant information. This will help you to build your database.

Don't forget to leave in the on-line publications if they are important and/or relevant in your field. After publication you can print out copies and send those out in your press kits as well. Put together a list of dream publications you would like to write for. Then develop a plan to getting published with them.

There are two types of people who are looking to write for publications. First are the professional writers who get paid for writing stories. Their compensation is a fixed dollar amount for each story they write. This is not what you are looking for as a speaker.

The speaker is the other kind of individual who writes for a publication. Speakers aren't looking for compensation "on the front end." They are looking to generate leads to a particular target market which the publication addresses.

Don't fall into the trap of writing to "get your name out into the market." This is a nebulous, unmeasurable concept. The compensation you are looking for as a speaker is a way to get those who read the articles you write to contact you and get them into your funnel. That means that they must allow you to put your contact information in the by-line. I would also make people a free offer of some sort to get them to respond.

The best example would be an offer like: "Call or email us to receive a free report on How to blah, blah, blah." If you make a compelling offer they will contact you. Your challenge is to trade them up the ladder. Some of the responders will eventually book you as a speaker.

Do not agree to take a writing assignment unless they put your contact information in the by-line as an absolute minimum. This becomes your form of payment.

Write Articles in Selected Publications

It will help your speaking business to get published. It will probably be easier for you to get published within niche market trade publications at first. Those are the publications that are put out by very specific individual industries. In my case, two of the ones I targeted were trade publications in the self storage industry.

But, if they offer to let you write an article for Fortune or Success, don't turn them down. But don't be waiting by the phone for a call. Not unless you have a book on the New York Times Best Seller list will these people be calling.

The first thing you need to do is to read the magazine that you want to write for. Sounds obvious, but many people don't do it. Read the publication and see how the articles are written in terms of both their style and substance.

The more you try to understand who their audience is, the better chance you will have of getting an article placed.

With the more general publications, my suggestion is to start small. Once you get articles published in the smaller regional and even local publications, your chances of landing the bigger and more prestigious publications will be increased. Larger publications like to see that you have already published in other smaller publications.

To get going at any size publication you need to first call the editor. You will find their name in the masthead of any publication that you are interested in writing for. Call them up only after you have read their publication and only if you have an idea in mind. You may end up having to "pitch" them right then and there. So be ready.

More likely than not, you will be asked a few questions to see if your background and concept for an article is of interest. Some editors won't be quite that kind. They will just get your name and address and send you their "package." This kit will give you a better idea of exactly what they are looking for and what their parameters are. READ IT.

Then follow up as instructed. Be persistent but not pushy.

In the beginning, you may not be able to make any demands. But soon after you get a few articles published you will need to make sure they you have your contact information in the by-line as a minimum. This would be your name, phone number and email address.

Include a good 8"x10" picture of yourself when you submit your article for publication. Most people will also want a picture in gif or jpg format. The sooner you get people to associate your name with your face, the better. This should be a professionally done "headshot." It should be black and white and you should have a few shots done in both casual and business attire. Take a look at pictures that you see in publications which you are looking to eventually get published in for some guidelines. Use a professional photographer if you have to. Their fee will be well worth it.

Later on, you will want to require that, in exchange for the article, the publication gives you the ability to put a "soft offer" in your by-line. This would be something like offering a free "report" or audio cassette on a topic of interest to anyone who will contact you. Your goal is to get the names of people who were interested in your article. This will help to build your database.

You can also offer people a free e-course. Get them to send you an email that subscribes them to an auto-responder series. Once again, webmarketingmagic can help you in this area.

When you try to promote your own events in a given industry, having written articles in their trade publications will increase your chances for success. Additionally, you may be invited by the associations in a given industry to speak at their conventions. If you don't get the invitations without asking, you may want to solicit them. More about that in another section of the book.

Save every article that you get published. It will help to build your PRESS KIT. If you get an article published in a magazine that you can buy off the newsstand, buy at least three or four copies immediately. Don't rely on their promise to send you copies. However well intentioned this promise may be, they frequently don't live up to them!

Keep one or two in a safe place that is well protected. You will want to use these copies as your "masters" when you go to get copies printed.

To get an idea of which publications you may want to work for, check out the "International Directory of Little Magazines and Small Presses." You can find it in most major libraries. Call your local library and ask if they carry it. Scan through it and start to make a list of where you want to get published.

Other Article Writing Opportunities

There are a number of other writing opportunities in which you could participate.

Some publications will allow you to write a guest essay. Look into the publications that you are interested in and see if they have a guest essayist on occasion. If they do, call the editor and ask them what criteria they use for your essay to be considered.

Letters to the editor are another place for you to try to get published. If you see an item in the news, make sure to respond quickly and succinctly to the publication. Don't be discouraged if you don't get published immediately. It may take time, but keep at it.

Newsletters

Newsletters are one way to keep in touch with people who are in your database. Sending out newsletters will help you to remind people of who you are and how good you were when you spoke.

The newsletters that you create and send need not be lengthy, but they do need to give people enough value that will make people want to read them every month. Whether its two pages or 32 pages, the information must keep them interested and deliver strong, interesting and useable information.

I have even seen a very effective newsletter on a normal-sized post-card. Very effective, unique and packed with good useable information. It works. Make it look good, but don't try to make it look too slick. You also have to decide whether or not you will charge people for your newsletter. Some speakers have two newsletters, one that's free and one they charge for.

Many speakers are now using e-zines. I like the idea of not having to pay for printing or postage. Check the section on internet marketing for more information on this topic.

Publicity

If you enjoy being a self promoter, your chances of success in the speaking business will be significantly enhanced. Publicity is a skill that can be learned. Learn it and you will be happy you did.

As opposed to advertising, publicity is free. Well, it's not really free. It will take a little bit of money and a fair amount of your time, but if you learn how to do it right, it will be 100% worth it.

Speaking engagements will come much easier when you get exposure in the media.

There are three primary forms of publicity I'd like to talk to you about: radio, TV, and print.

When people see you on TV or hear you on the radio, you will rarely get a call where someone will want to book you as a speaker.

Your goal from any media appearances will be to generate leads and "get people into your funnel." Getting them into your database will allow you to sell them products and trade them up your ladder.

Very seldom will someone make a $5,000 decision without first making a much smaller and less-expensive decision. This means that your goal with media appearances is to get people to call you. From that point on, you will try to trade them up to more expensive products and eventually a certain number of buyers will use you as a speaker.

Understanding that your goal is to get people into your database, your media appearances must include an offer to give people something for free. This free offer must be perceived as being something of significant value. People will not respond to free offers if they're not worth having.

I will sometimes make a free offer but charge a nominal fee for postage, like $2. If you make it a completely free offer, not only will you not cover your costs, but you will have every Tom, Dick and Harry respond to your offer. Many of these folks will not be qualified. Even at the $2 level, you will still get a lot of "chaff", but you will still have a lot of wheat.

My assumption here is that you are dealing with a mass market. If you are doing PR within a tightly niched market, you can make totally free offers without worrying about getting a flood of unqualified respondents.

Your free offer should be something like a "free report." The key in your offering is something that is very low cost to you but has a very high perception of value to those who are responding. The key to getting a good flood of responses is the title that you use. Make the title as seductive, benefit laden, and interesting as you can. Making a free offer will make it easier for you to get media coverage.

To summarize: you offer something for free to generate leads. You put those leads into your database. You then try to sell them products. Once they buy your less expensive products you trade them "up the ladder" of your products to the more expensive ones. A certain number of those who buy products will eventually use you as a speaker. Even if they don't, you'll make plenty of money off them in product sales or consulting work.

Radio

I recently recorded a program on how to get on radio and sell your products with a good friend of mine, Alex Carroll. If you like the idea of getting on radio, go to www.radiopublicity.com. Here are some of the highlights.

First, remember the radio show producer's goal is to give their listeners something of value that will make them want to tune in and, as a result, boost their ratings. Keep this in mind when you approach the radio market. They are not interested in what you want; they have their own agenda. If you can help them achieve their goals, they will help you achieve yours.

First, you will need to get a list of radio stations and producers at those stations who would have an interest in your topic. You don't want to approach the home and garden producer with a business topic.

After you have narrowed your list to producers at those stations who would have an interest in your topic, get them on the phone. They can usually be reached if you are persistent. But don't expect them to give you a whole lot of their time. So be ready with a very effective 20 second pitch that summarizes your agenda.

Be prepared to sell them when they start asking you some questions. This conversation might basically turn into the pre-interview, which usually occurs at a later time. Go with it and do the best job you can. They will then ask you to send them something. You will then send them your press kit (discussed elsewhere in this book), and then follow up to get booked.

Once you are booked, make sure you do a great job. Do your part and the host and producer will help you promote yourself and your free offer to fill your funnel with leads.

Radio TV Interview Report

This is a great publication run by two friends of mine, Stephe Hall and Bill Harrison.

It is a publication that goes out every 10 days to the producers of radio and TV shows highlighting interesting potential guests. It is a great way to get your name in front of a lot of producers quickly and efficiently.

You can purchase various size ads for a set period of time. Producers look through this publication and then call you when they see something that interests them.

If you want to get on radio, you should be in this publication. For free information call Bill Harrison at 800-989-1400 extension 121. Most of the people they deal with are book publishers. So call them AFTER you finish your book.

They are also most appropriate if you have a mass market consumer topic. Business to business topics would not be appropriate. You can also visit their website at RTIR.com.

Exposure in this publication will dramatically increase your chances of getting booked on radio shows. Being on radio will significantly increase your chances of having someone buy your books, and of you getting booked as a speaker.

TV

Many speakers concentrate their efforts on generating TV interviews. This is misguided unless you can land a spot on Oprah.

The problem is that very few TV programs will allow you to make a free offer and publicize it using a toll free number. It is absolutely absurd that TV folks won't make a great offer available to their audience this way, but they won't.

Occasionally TV will let you make an offer like this when you have a non-profit cause that is politically correct and that they support.

If you have a free report on how to prevent child abuse, they will definitely give out your 800 number.

I think that's great, but why shouldn't they do their viewers a service and allow other products and services of interest to be promoted in a similar fashion?

It's a nice philosophical argument, but the reality is that it ain't gonna happen.

So TV might be good for your ego, but in MOST cases it is a waste of time and energy on your part. Shows will sometimes allow links from their websites to yours, but it is still not nearly as good as getting them to put your 800 number on the screen.

If you want to pursue TV, the system is similar to radio. You contact the producers and then send them material. I would rather you put yourself in a situation where people come to you as a result of your book or other media appearances which are easier to get.

Once again, the folks at RTIR have an excellent product for this purpose. Call Bill Harrison at 1-800-989-1400 extension 121.

Print

Getting print media coverage is primarily based on your ability to write a great press release. Remember, you don't want your press release to be picked up and run "as is." You want the reporter to be sufficiently interested to call you and hopefully do a longer and more in-depth story. The key to a great press release is a great headline.

Your Headline

This is the most important part of your release. A media person has got to see it and be intrigued enough to want to call you.

After you write the headline, you need to ask yourself: "So what?" If you ask yourself this question about the headline and you can't come up with a good headline, change it. It isn't working.

A great headline will make an unbelievable claim. This creates an immediate visceral reaction by a media person. Some may think you are full of it. Others will want to expose you as a fraud. Whatever happens, they will react. Not like most of the press releases they see. Most produce no reaction whatsoever which becomes the kiss of death.

When you write your headline, make an unbelievable claim that you can prove. If you can't prove the outrageous claim you made, you're dead. And you will never get the media's attention again. You'll be branded a liar. No second chance.

It also helps to send a release that ties in well with a current event. Timing here is everything.

Taking a story that everyone is going with and coming at it in a novel way will help you get coverage. Reporters are looking for a new way to approach the same story.

Always look to present a different angle on any story you attack.

Another big problem is being too serious. Frequently you can attack the story in a funny way and have a much better chance of getting coverage. Making your release fun and funny increases your chance of getting coverage.

In your release it helps to offer a giveaway. It doesn't have to be something that costs a great deal, but it should be something of high perceived value. This usually means a free report or booklet. High perceived value and low cost to you: make it something they will want to keep.

Don't tell people you will give them something of value and then bait and switch them. If you give them sales material about your business, you will get a strong backlash. Make the item you give away something that you can tie to your advertising for a one-two punch.

Now the dilemma of how to get the item from your hands to theirs. There are many ways to do this. The most costly is obviously with an 800 number that people call to get the item. The problem with this approach is that some people will call to get anything as long as it's free. If you ask people to call the 800 number you will pay for the call and the postage to get the item to people.

You could then use a non 800-number and still pay for the postage. This would still be more expensive than your cheapest option. That would be to ask people to enclose their own stamped self addressed envelope and have them respond to a non-800 number.

There are different schools of thought on this one. If you make it easier and cheaper for people to respond, the quality of the leads will be lower. But, you'll get more respondents. The other way is to make it tougher and more expensive for people to get the free "stuff." Doing it this way will give you higher quality leads who will be more apt to buy the more expensive stuff you try to sell them.

Don't write a headline that says something terminally boring about your business like: "ABC Company Announces 2nd Quarter Profits Up 17%." This does not pass the "So What" test. No one cares.

You can send the exact same releases to any size media outlet. Big or small, use the exact same approach.

The Body Copy of the Press Release has Three Parts.

Part 1: This is the first/opening paragraph. It should contain all of the important information you want to convey. This may be as far as the program director will read. You want to hook the reader as soon as possible. You want to make it so that they can get the entire story just from this one paragraph. Stick to just the hard facts.

Part 2: Include some quotations and credentials about the person making the quote: Most often YOU! "The theory that 97% of all restaurants waste their money on advertising is true, says Fred Gleeck, restaurant marketing consultant." This quote would not go in the first section. It is a supporting statement. The quote supports the information provided in the first section.

Part 3: This wraps up the release and provides contact information.

Becoming Famous

If you want to be a highly successful speaker, you must dedicate yourself to achieving fame. In order to become famous, these are the critical things you must do. You must be published. This means you need to write a book on your topic. Second, you must get your articles published in magazines. Third, you must get the media machine working.

Fame will be one of the most important elements of you getting to land speaking engagements. Don't act like it's not important. It's critical to your success. Learn how to become famous and your speaking business will thrive. Unfortunately, this is true regardless of your level of talent as a speaker.

Creating Your Press Kit

When you go out to generate press and publicity, you will need to have a "package" to send people. The items that I list for you in this section should all be put into a nice package called a presentation folder.

Press Release

A copy of your press release as described in the publicity section should always be in your press kit.

Fact Sheet

A fact sheet is a very factual description of yourself and your services. This should list all of the relevant facts about you and your business. I would characterize this as a bio-plus.

Brochure

If you have a brochure for your speaking business, include it. This, in addition to your one page faxable sheet, should be included in your kit. It should be packed with benefits, not features.

Interview

If you haven't been interviewed by a major media outlet, then you need to create your own interview and include it in your press kit. Ask the major questions that you would think people would want to know about you and your speaking services and include it in this interview piece.

Q&A

Also include a one page sheet where you give answers to the 20 or more most important questions in your field of expertise.

Testimonials

Any glowing letters that people have written about you should be included in your press kit as well. If you have lots of them, put the most impressive and most recent ones in and leave out the rest.

Client List

If you are just starting out and don't have any clients, volunteer to speak for a certain number of people who will agree to give you a great letter of recommendation and appear on your client list. Invoice them after the fact with your full rates on the invoice. Then put a big slash through it and mark it "fee waived." This will let them know what you consider to be the full value of your speaking services.

Photos

Like I mentioned earlier, you will also need some black and white headshots and a few action shots as well.

Continuing Education Opportunities

In many cities around the country, there are opportunities for you to do presentations at your local continuing education centers. I highly recommend you take advantage of these opportunities. This is not just something the beginning speaker should do. Veterans can benefit as well.

In large cities like New York, Chicago, and others, they have catalogs that sit in vending devices in various strategic locations around the city.

In other cities, classes are held at local community colleges. If you are having trouble finding them, call your local college or university. Talk to their continuing education department. Ask them who there is in your market in addition to themselves who do continuing education classes.

You won't make a lot of money doing these, but you will get a great place to practice. You'll be able to practice both your presentations and product sales. Presenting in your own city also makes it simple and easy for you to do.

As compensation they normally give you around 15% of the total revenue generated. In my case, when you add that to my product sales, I rarely make less than $1000 for three hours in an evening. This is not big money, but I am basically getting paid to practice.

In addition, I don't have to get on an airplane. As a seasoned speaker, trust me, that's nice. The way to get them to book you is to use the following system

Step 1

Get the name of the person who is the "program director" or the person who decides on who teaches.

Step 2

Send them a letter.

1ST PAGE

1ST PARAGRAPH

Personalize the letter. Say that you are submitting the following materials to see if it might be included in their course catalog.

2ND PARAGRAPH

In Bold: Course Title, Sub Title, One sentence description of the class.

3RD PARAGRAPH

The rationale for why you should be presenting to the class. Also, why it would be of benefit to the people who would take the class.

4TH PARAGRAPH

The rationale for why you should be the only one to present this class. Your experience, credentials, stuff you publish on the topic (newsletter, set of tapes, that you do a public seminar, your book, etc.)

2ND PAGE

COURSE DESCRIPTION

Basically, design them an ad as they would put in their catalog. Make it short and snappy. Give it a compelling title and a great description. Keep the description to a maximum of 200 words. Use bullet points for the hot stuff.

3RD PAGE

YOUR BIO

Everything and anything you can put in to make you look like the guru on the topic. A resume that exactly fits the class you want to teach. This will be different for each class: film different from video, different from consulting, etc.

4TH PAGE

APPENDIX

Any and everything you have to back up all of your claims. Letters of recommendation, press releases, etc., possibly even a set of materials — books and tapes (for video, send them a set of product). Also a video of you doing a presentation, if possible, but it's not essential.

Step 3
Follow up to ask them if they got the stuff, but don't become a pest.

Step 4

Contact all the continuing ed places in your area, not just one! Get this list from LERN (Manhattan, KS)

Trade Shows

There are two ways that trade shows are relevant to speakers. One is the trade shows of your peers. This would be any and all events where other speakers, trainers, or consultants attend. After all, you are now in each one of these categories.

Some people spend an awful lot of time attending these kinds of events. My suggestion is to spend no more than three or four days each year attending events for you and your peers.

Two reasons why. First, you should be spending your precious time making money rather than spending it. Second, the more time you spend at these meetings the more your peers will wonder why you're there and not out working. This second one is a perception issue, but it is worth mentioning, because it is important.

I attend many trade shows in the niche markets where I do a great deal of speaking. If you start niching yourself like I recommend, you should start doing the same. This is time worth spending if you have a very specific agenda when you go.

The first question will always be whether or not you should get a booth. My answer is only if you are a speaker at the event. I don't stick to this rule myself these days, but that is because I am expected to be at the trade shows in certain industries.

Your first choice is to get the organization that is putting on the trade show to book you as a featured speaker. If you can't get the featured speaker position, you should still accept a breakout session if they offer it.

As you get further along in your speaking career, it may only be worth it to you to take the featured speaker slot. To compute how much the speech will be worth, you need to combine your fee and the approximate amount of product sales that you can generate.

When you first get started, the best way to get booked as a speaker is to do two things: write articles in the trade publications, and try to get the association executives to hear you speak at some other venue.

The last time I was booked to speak as a featured speaker at a convention in one of my niche markets, I gave a one hour speech. I then proceeded to sell a total of over $32,000 worth of product.

This particular organization didn't give me a speaking fee for the event. Do you think I cared? Obviously not with these numbers.

Personal Contact Marketing

This is my fancy term for networking in the 21st century.

I end up getting over 40% of my business using the strategies that I am about to lay out to you here.

The secret to successful networking revolves around follow-up. Without follow up, you will not succeed as a networker.

Whenever I meet someone, I immediately follow up with a hand-written note. If you think this technique was effective before, it is even more effective in the high-tech internet and email era. People are actually shocked when you send them a personal handwritten note after you meet them.

If I meet them on a plane I will literally write the note on the next flight (if I had to connect). When I get back to my office, their name is immediately entered into my database, ACT! In the case of personal contact, I enter them into ACT as opposed to just getting their email address.

I will then follow up with a phone call about 10 days later. The person will take my call in 90% of the cases. Why? Because they at least owe me the courtesy of speaking to me after I sent them such a nice handwritten note.

If they are not the proper contact for me to pursue from a speaking business standpoint, they will usually tell me who to call.

I then do a traditional follow up campaign. Depending on how likely they are to buy, I send them different promotional material. The more likely I feel they are to buy, the more I will send them. Again, don't jump the gun and send all of the people you meet all of your expensive promotional materials. You can always send them more when you see they have an interest.

The probability of selling a particular person you meet through your "personal contact marketing" is almost always related to where you met them. Those people I meet on airplanes or at airports seem to be the most likely to eventually use my services.

I attribute this to those individuals having the right demographics.

Where should you network? Everywhere. You can never tell where your next speaking engagement will come from.

Speaking Mechanics

Three Characteristics of a Great Speaker

People are much more apt to buy products from someone who is perceived as a great speaker, everything else being equal.

Over the three years I did CareerTrack seminars, I did a survey "on the sly." I would ask participants at these events to write down what they thought were the three most important characteristics of a great speaker.

I did not give them any other coaching. I just asked that question and repeated it exactly the same way if they didn't quite hear it right. Over the course of a year I did this informal survey many times and got a total of about 2500 responses to this question.

They would write down their answers on a slip of paper and hand them to me at the end of the seminar.

I compiled the results and this is how they came out. Although there were other answers, these three were at the top and in this order. All other answers accounted for less than 20% of the total answers.

Sincerity

Top on the list was sincerity. People want a speaker, I believe, that they feel is "real." There is nothing that turns people off quicker than someone acting, or speaking like someone they aren't.

Everyone knows this intuitively; the question is how do we create sincerity? What are the behavioral manifestations of sincerity? When people say "That speaker really meant what he/she was saying," what caused them to say and think that? I have found three elements to be the greatest contributants to what we all know and perceive as sincerity.

First, you must speak in a conversational tone, a tone that people will feel is how you normally talk as a person in your every day life.

This is one of the reasons I think that Oprah and Hugh Downs are successful. When you listen to them, you get the feeling that they really are the people that you hear and see on TV.

If you want an example of this, take Lou Heckler, one of my favorite professional speakers. He is REAL PEOPLE personified! If you don't know who he is, you should. Call NSA and get one of his tapes.

Another necessary ingredient in conveying sincerity is to speak only about topics you really believe in and feel passionate about. Those speakers who can "talk about anything" will fall flat on their face in this area. There is no way anyone can truly feel passionate about everything (or anything) they speak about.

The last area in which one needs to convey what others will perceive as sincerity is comfort and an in-depth knowledge of the material. You really need to know what you are talking about in order to be perceived as sincere. This means that whatever your topic, you need to be an eager and interested student.

I have always had a passion for marketing. I read every book, attend every seminar, and buy every tape on the subject. Over the past 10 years I have spent over $100,000 in my study of marketing. When I speak on this topic, one of the things that contributes to my being perceived as sincere is my passion as well as knowledge about the topic.

For you, this means picking a topic area that you really enjoy, studying it, and reading everything you can about it. Know the field inside and out. Keep current with the latest trends and ideas. If you try to do all of this with a topic and find it to be drudgery, you are not speaking in the right topic area.

Someone talked to me not long ago about what they were going to do when they retire. I don't understand retirement. If you love what you do, shouldn't you want to do it forever? My Dad is now 87. He has written 17 books since the age of 65. He couldn't have done this unless he loved to write. If I live to the same age, I am sure I will still be a serious student of marketing.

Content

Second on the survey that people filled out for me was content. People do not want to listen to a speaker who doesn't deliver solid, useable information. How does one ensure that this happens? With a few simple steps.

First, you need to deliver information that is non-theoretical. It must be information that is practical and easily applied. You should make it crystal clear as to how people use this information. Give them all the tools. Nothing should be left to chance. At the end of your seminar or speech, people should not be left thinking, "OK, what do I do now?"

You have got to give them the steps to follow, preferably in a handout that details everything they need to do. If you have ever bought a product that needs assembly, just think about how you have felt when the directions they included were poor. If you give poor direction to your audience on the HOW TO DO IT side, they will judge you as weak in the area of content.

In order to make sure that your content is applied, you need to hang each of your major points on a hook. In addition to your handout, you need to tell a story, or give an example that people will remember. Some "anchor" has got to be present to give your audience a chance to store the concept and be able to retrieve it later quickly and easily. Stories and examples are the best and most memorable hooks. People will often remember the story and then remember the content point many years after your encounter with them.

Everyone learns differently. Make sure you understand this when you are trying to give your great content retention value. Some people will need to see something — perhaps some kind of a prop or visual aid. Others will need to hear something to remember it. The story idea works well. Still others will need to apply the concept in order to remember the content point. Create an exercise where they have to do something so they'll remember it.

Ideally if you have three points that you want to cover in a speech, you can deliver these three content points and illustrate them each three ways, one for each of the different kinds of learners in the audience.

Humor

In my survey, the third most important characteristic of a good speaker was humor. There are three key things you need to do to make your speech or seminar more humorous.

Any and all humor you use is best when it is self-deprecating. Make yourself the butt of all the jokes you use. This will endear you to the audience. It shows you have confidence in yourself to show people that you screw up. You can never make a mistake and offend anyone if you pick on yourself.

Remember, only a Catholic can tell a joke that seems to make Catholics look foolish. Anyone else will appear to be insensitive and bigoted.

To be funny you need to tell stories, not tell jokes. If you tell a joke and it doesn't work, everyone knows it. No one laughs. And with a joke, there is no getting around the fact that it didn't work. When you set up a joke, everyone knows what that set-up looks like. They also know what people thought of the joke by the amount of laughter you get.

There is an easy way to be safe on this one. Tell stories! When you tell what you think to be a funny story and no one laughs, everyone will just think it was a story. The joke set-up telegraphs to everyone that what comes next is supposed to be funny. If people don't laugh at the joke, it will be looked at as a joke that didn't work. This is not true with a story. If it is funny, people will laugh. If it isn't, it will just seem like another story. Less harm done.

This leads to the last point I'll make on humor. IT'S ONLY FUNNY IF THEY LAUGH. The definition of funny must come from the people receiving the message. I don't care if you think a joke is funny. I don't care if your family thinks it is funny. It is NOT funny if people don't laugh.

If you try a story attempting to be funny and it doesn't get a laugh, then you need to drop the story, that is if you are looking to be funny using that particular story. Your audience is the only true judge of humor.

If you are looking to add humor to your speeches, use self-deprecating stories. As you speak, "take notes" on which ones work (audiences laugh) and which ones don't. Drop those stories which don't and try new ones in their place.

Comedians do it this way. They start with say 100 jokes. When then deliver them, people might laugh at five of them. They keep the five and then add 95 new ones. Of the 95 new ones, people might laugh at six of those. The comedian will then keep those six that work. He/she now has 11 jokes that work. They then repeat the process.

I'm not saying that you should become a comedian on stage. But I am saying that my survey tells us that if you want to be considered a great speaker, you have to be perceived as funny. This doesn't mean that every story you tell has to be funny, but if you follow the steps above, at least more of them will, thus enhancing your chances of being perceived as a better speaker and helping you to sell more products.

Sincere Self Disclosure

A highly effective means of getting people on your side when you do a seminar or speech is to do some baring of your soul.

This will help you to connect with the audience. The problem is that you walk a very thin line when you tell the audience information about your personal life. If you do a certain amount of it, it will work well. If you go beyond a certain point, you can blow it.

I have been in presentations where speakers went well beyond the bounds of propriety when telling information about themselves.

Where you draw the line is very situationally dependent. If you are in a seminar on child abuse, you would be able to be much more self-disclosive than at a business seminar. This kind of seminar lends itself to people talking about themselves and their individual situations.

Business seminars, on the other hand, are not the place to talk about very explicit personal matters, unless you have specifically designed the seminar that way and promoted it as such.

The bottom line is that it's fine to let people know who you are, but don't go beyond the bounds of what seems sensible given the type of speech or seminar you are giving.

Improvisational Comedy

If you want to take one kind of class that will benefit you immensely in the speaking business, my suggestion would be to take an
"improv" class. When you see people who are good at "thinking on
their feet" they are probably fairly accomplished improvisational
actors. This may be true without their even knowing it.

This is an area where some people are gifted with a certain amount
of natural, innate ability. No matter how bad you think you are in
this area, don't worry, everyone can improve. The question is the
degree of improvement. Some people can be transformed into
comedic improv geniuses, whereas the rest of us mere mortals can
only get marginally better.

Regardless of which one of these categories you fall into, take a class.
You can find them at just about any school that offers acting classes. After you take one, email me with your thoughts. I'd like to hear
how it went.

I would not, however, recommend that you take a traditional acting
class. I think it actually can hurt you as a speaker. The goal of a
speaker should be to come off as real as possible. Traditional acting
classes don't have this as their goal. I would skip them.

Other speakers may disagree with me, but having been cast in two
films (one with a lead part), I think I can speak from experience. And
no, I will not tell you the names of the films. They were pretty
cheesy "B" action films that I would rather see destroyed!

Taking Care of Your Voice

As a speaker, you need to take care of your voice. It's like a professional pianist. Without a piano, they can't make a living. Yet it is
surprising how little energy is exerted by speakers to take care of
their most important asset: their voice.

This is another very important reason why speakers need to diver-
sify into products. Let's say that you lost the use of your voice
permanently ... what would you do?

Here are some suggestions about taking care of your voice. Many of
these items were told to me many years back by a speaker named
Roger Burgraff.

Treat your vocal cords very gingerly. Never yell or scream. This is very damaging to your vocal cords.

Always use a mike when speaking to more than 30 or 40 people. I have tried to be MACHO on occasions and belted out my message without using one. One time I did a full day seminar without a mike. What a huge mistake. My throat was sore for three days. It completely freaked me out. From then on, never again did I try to appear like an oratorical big-shot and not use a mike. This was just plain stupid on my part. Don't make the same error.

Throughout a long presentation you need to keep water by your side and keep hydrating your vocal cords. The best analogy I can think of is trying to run a car without oil. I did this with my first car in college and it died on me. The same thing will happen to your voice if you don't keep putting fluid down your throat.

It should not be coffee or any caffeine item either, but just water, preferably at room temperature and with some lemon, if you want.

An interesting aside here was that I was on the road for four years with CareerTrack. In that time I rarely got sick. I attribute it to the amount of water and lemon I drank when I did my full day seminars.

It will make it so you have to use the bathroom fairly frequently, so plan your breaks and group exercises accordingly.

When you aren't speaking, try not to talk. Don't speak over the radio or sing in the car. Avoid talking on the phone as well.

Also, avoid eating dairy products before you speak, it creates mucus.

Alcohol is out as well.

When you clear your throat, do it carefully. Don't do it forcefully as you see many people do. This again will harm your vocal cords.

You may also want to go to your local health food store and pick up some Echiynacea. Take it straight or put it into tea. Also look for a product called "Throat Coat." It is a tea that they sell over the counter. It's a great way to treat your throat in the evening before and after a speaking engagement.

Sprays for your voice are OK and lozenges can't hurt you either. Try to get the ones that are sugar free.

To determine the optimum pitch you should be using when you speak, start humming. Then throw in a word. This tells you at what pitch level you should be speaking so as not to hurt your vocal cords.

Microphones

When speaking to any group over 30 or 40, you need to be using a mike. If not, you will ruin your voice. When it comes to mikes you have choices. You can either use a hand held mike or a lavaliere mike (with or without a cord). A lavaliere mike is the one that you see on most people on television. It's the small microphone that clips on to your lapel.

Regardless of any choice that you make regarding a microphone, make sure that there is ALWAYS a back-up mike available. It has happened to every speaker at least once or twice. You are about to speak to a large group of people anxious to hear from you. All of a sudden, the mike goes out. YIKES!

If you use a lot of overheads or do anything where you need to use your hands, a lavaliere mike is a better choice.

Using a lavaliere is good in some ways and bad in others. By definition, the distance between your mouth and the microphone remains constant. This means you will not be able to do certain things that will contribute to creating something called vocal variety.

This is why singers always use a hand held microphone. When was the last time you saw a singer with a lavaliere mike? Watch some of the great singers when they sing. You will see them moving the mike closer or further from their mouth during the song. They do this to create a different feel as they sing. Successful speakers do the same. I recommend that you use a hand held mike for the precise reasons I just mentioned.

Whichever type of microphone you use, travel with your own mike, whatever your primary choice is. It is well worth your money to be completely comfortable with your speaking instrument and how it behaves. Using a different mike every time you speak is like driving a different car every day. You can't gain any level of comfort or feel.

I travel with a hand held cordless mike manufactured by Samson. I don't make a specific recommendation that you use that particular brand, but I have nothing against them.

Use a Remote/Cordless Mike

Whether you choose to go with a hand-held or lavaliere, I would always suggest you go with one that is cordless or remote.

This will allow you not to be trapped behind the podium, allowing you to go into the audience if it makes sense to do so.

If and when you do mingle with your audience members, try not to make it seem completely contrived and scripted. The best example I can think of is if you have ever seen Elizabeth Dole give a speech. Although I think that going into the audience is a great way to "mix it up" with the audience, her method is a great example of something that looks contrived.

You know that she is going to do it. She telegraphs her intentions to do so. It makes the action itself look rehearsed and unnatural, just the opposite of what a speaker should be trying to achieve with the action.

Make sure that, if and when you venture into the audience, you make it seem like you're doing it naturally.

Scripting Your Presentation

I am not a believer in exact scripting for presentations. I believe in outlining.

After I have been giving a certain speech or module for a while, I start to use the same lines over and over, but I do not start out by writing the entire speech word for word. Some people do. This isn't wrong. It just isn't my style. If it works for you, do it.

It only works if you can not make it sound like your presentation is canned. When it sounds scripted, you know it's not working!

Those who do choose to write out every word often appear as if they have done that when they speak. It looks stilted.

My preference is a detailed outline. I then give this speech in smaller venues before I roll it out at a "real" speaking event. That's why I still give the occasional "free" speech and continue to do the occasional continuing education event.

This allows me to practice.

Effective Opening and Closing Techniques

There is a principle in psychology called the primacy-recency effect. To give it to you in a nutshell, people remember most, what they heard first and what they heard last. What they heard last has a slight edge in all the tabulations.

What does that mean to you as a speaker? That these two points of your presentation are absolutely crucial to your success.

A speaker who doesn't know how to effectively open and close will never be a mega success in the speaking business.

Openings

Whenever you do a seminar, don't do what 90% of seminar leaders and speakers do. As a group, most seminar leaders will spend the first few minutes discussing all of the minutia of the administrative elements. This would include telling people where the bathrooms are and when the breaks will be held.

The job of your opening is to capture peoples' attention from the moment you start to speak. The worst way to do this is to give all of the embarrassing administrative elements at the very start.

The analogy to this would be movies that start by running the title and actors first. Again, take a look at The French Connection for how to do it right.

Although I love spontaneity, you need to have your opening rehearsed extremely well. It should be so well memorized and rehearsed that it doesn't sound like it is.

The reason why you want to have it so well rehearsed is because it is so important for you to start out with your audience on a positive note. If you are nervous, you don't want to have to think too much.

Should you have only one opening? Not unless you only do one speech. And even then, you will get bored doing the same opening every time, in addition to the fact that if you ever speak to the same group again, they will be even more bored than you are.

Whatever opening you select to use, and you should have a number to choose from, make sure your audience can see it's relevance to them as a group.

There is nothing worse than a great opening where everyone looks at themselves as if to say: "That was clever, but what does it have to do with us?" As you read great books and watch good movies, note how they open. See what you like and try to duplicate it in form and substance.

A number of openings to consider are to:

Read a Children's Book

I thought this one would be pretty hokey until a friend of mine with a three year old gave me one of her books to read. The next day I used it to open a seminar. The name of the book is "Miranda" and it was perfect to illustrate what I wanted the audience to see.

Use a Song

This isn't one I would ever do, but those of you with a great voice may want to consider this one. Remember, it can't be just any song, it has to be relevant to your message.

I wanted to use a Reggae song by an artist named Jimmy Cliff. His song is "You Can Get It If You Really Want." I wasn't going to sing it, but I wish I could have gotten the rights to use it at a reasonable rate. Unfortunately, what they wanted to charge me was way too much. But it's still a great song.

Fables or Stories

Another common way to open a speech or seminar is with a fable or story. Once again, not just any story, but one which is captivating and relevant.

Unfinished Story

The unfinished story is a clever technique that can work very well. If you get partially through an interesting story and then don't finish it, people will be waiting to hear the rest. When done correctly, it will work extremely well to keep their interest.

Something Physical

Can you find a way to open your seminar with a bang? Literally? If it's appropriate to your message, it might be wise to see if you can. Any opening you use should get people's attention, and be relevant to your topic.

Closings

This is potentially the most important part of your speech. According to the data, it is the most memorable.

Quotes

Many quotes are regularly used to close a speech or seminar. Some are appropriate, some are not. If you use a quote, it should be appropriate and relevant to your preceding speech. It is also much better that you don't use a quote that has been heard many times before.

The Rest of Your Unfinished Story

If you used an unfinished story to open your speech, you will want to finish it with your closing. If you don't, people will be really confused.

Poems

The right poem may be an appropriate closing. I have used one that I learned many years ago to close a program a few times. I would only use it for certain types of groups when absolutely appropriate.

Whatever you choose as a closing, it must be memorable, hopefully in a positive way. It is also acceptable to close with a challenge or a summary of what you have told the group.

Closing Your Programs Effectively

I have a number of standard closings that I use and that I know work. Keeping in mind that people will remember this more than anything else about your presentation, make sure you've got a proven winner to close with.

It would be a good idea to have numerous closings so that you can decide which to use "on the fly", if necessary, based on the audience composition and your feel for the group.

If you're just starting out, you need to test. You will be testing locally to see what works. Inventory the closings that work well. Perfect them until you know exactly how to use them and how they will work.

Your best closing device is the story, either about you or about someone else. The story should take your main theme for the presentation and neatly wrap things up. Make certain that this story proves your most important point. This is what people will remember most.

In many situations, it may be appropriate to end on a "call to action" for your audience. This will depend on circumstances, but if you use this technique, make it very clear what you are asking them to do.

Customization of Speech and Seminar Content

There are various levels of customization that you can do to your speech or seminar. The greater the level of this customization, the more time it will take and the more you will have to charge.

If your client is willing to foot this bill, then by all means do it. It has been my experience that 90% of clients will want a little bit of customization, but very few will pay for the maximum level.

I would separate customization into three separate categories.

The lowest level of customizing I would call "making mention". This would be where you make a casual reference at a few points in time to the organization and any particular individuals within the company or organization.

Your intermediate level of customization I would call "integration". In addition to the above, you would also talk to a number of people in your audience in advance of the session and use some of their examples.

The highest level of customization I would characterize as "immersion". This is where you do all of the above and also create exercises that would take real life situations that attendees are facing right now and use them in your presentation.

Pricing for these different levels is difficult when you first start. You won't know how much time it will take you, so you'll just have to guess. Sometimes your work will take much more time than anticipated. On other occasions you will get things done much more quickly than expected.

In most cases, when your clients agree to some level of customization, you will find them wanting the middle option 80% of the time. At least this is true for me. As with most things, when you provide people with three viable options, they usually choose the middle one.

Adjusting Your Level as a Speaker

As a speaker, you will talk to certain groups differently than you will talk to others. If you are talking to a group of union members your approach should be different than if you are talking to the board of directors of the same company.

Does this mean you don't feel that the union folks are as good as people? Absolutely not. But you must speak to people in a language and form that they will relate to and understand.

I never talk down to people. Folks who have "lower level" jobs are often highly intelligent. I just want to make sure that, whenever I speak to a group, I connect with the largest number of group members.

Audience Composition

Depending on the composition of your audience, you may have to adjust your presentation. If you have a lot of factory workers, your style and manner will be very different than speaking to a collection of CEOs.

Although we are always told to "treat everyone alike," in this case that would be absurd. The problems and issues of one group aren't the same as the other.

When putting together your presentation for a group, make sure you understand who in the group will affect how you deliver your information, (even more reason for you to talk to a number of people who will be in the audience before you do your speech).

Handling Different Group Sizes

The way you speak to a group of 2,000 people is very different than how you should speak to a group of 35 or 40. Speakers who would tell you it's all the same are deluded. It can't be; the dynamics of a small groups are much different than those of a large group.

I have spoken to groups of all sizes over the last 15 years and have found that you need to approach each group size differently.

Let me give you some specific suggestions for dealing with each of the following group sizes.

Small Groups: 25 or Less

With a group this small it is often weird for you to be standing and having your participants seated. You can certainly stand part of the time during your presentation when you get up to write things on an easel or white board, but it wouldn't seem appropriate to be standing the entire time.

A group this small requires that you create more of a boardroom atmosphere, an atmosphere more like that of a corporate board meeting. You will serve as the moderator or chairman.

With a group this size you will not be using a mike.

It is also imperative with a group this size that you get them involved immediately. Give them ways to contribute to the entire group and also within smaller groups that you break them down into.

When you create groups within a small group of this size, try to separate those people who work together. They will have a tendency to want to be in the same group. This will not make your efforts as meaningful.

Medium Groups: 25 – 100

When you speak to groups of this size, you will probably have to use a mike, both for the sake of your voice and for group control purposes.

In this size group you should break people into groups of four to six at the very start of your session. Appoint a group leader and change that leader periodically. In a group this size, it is difficult to have participants change groups, but if you can do it once, it will break up the time you spend with them.

When you give them exercises to do, mingle with the groups physically. Listen, but don't talk. Give them some positive feedback, but don't inject yourself into the group. You are merely the moderator.

Large Groups: 100 – 2000

Depending on how large your group is, you may or may not be able to do any interacting with your crowd.

If you are not on a stage and it's relatively easy to travel into the audience, make some trips. This will obviously mean that you must have a cordless mike. Go out into the group for a purpose.

If you ask a question of a participant, don't give them the mike; you will lose control. Hold the mike as they answer.

This is where your improvisational skills will come in very handy.

If you are doing a one day presentation with a group of this size, groups will be essential to create. They will allow you to manage a group of this size with relative ease.

One of the biggest problems will be getting the group's attention back. Use the following technique to do it. Let your group know at the beginning of your time together that you will use a technique to get their attention back and that you need their help.

Tell them that when you want to get their focus back, you will raise your hand. When any of them see your hand raised, they should also raise their hand. Before long, everyone will see hands raised and stop talking and give you back the floor. This is incredibly effective for getting the attention of a large group back quickly and easily.

Rallies: 2000+

When you speak to large groups of this size you will generally be up on a stage. Your chances for one on one interaction will be severely limited.

This is where your ability to create empathy and connect with your audience will be the most challenging. Even though you are speaking to such a large group, keep reminding yourself that you are trying to talk to them individually. Think of one person as you speak.

Never take on a speaking engagement of this nature unless you are supremely confident with your speaking skills and subject matter. This is not the time to practice or to try out any new material or ideas.

Your ability to sell products to a group of this size will be to show them how much useable content you can give them in a short period of time.

Testing Speech/Seminar Material

I will never forget a conversation I had with a fairly well known speaker a few years back at a convention. I was thinking of using an idea that I had come up with in a speech. It was something I had never seen done by another speaker and I was excited to use the concept.

I shared the idea with him. His response was lukewarm at best. He was basically concerned that I would use something so different and unusual. Either that or he liked the idea so much he was going to steal it, which happens all the time among speakers!

My idea is to take a concept like this and test it in a smaller venue, where you aren't risking it with one of your major clients in front of thousands of people. But without new material being tested constantly, you will become stagnant. Your speeches will get very old and uninteresting.

This is the precise reason why I still like doing presentations at continuing education centers.

Topic Files for Each of Your Topics

You need to keep a file for each of your topics. Any time you are reading a book or magazine or watching television you need to capture the information and drop it into the file. Put any and everything related to your topic in this file.

Periodically you need to review this file and see what you can add to make your speeches and seminars more meaty and interesting. Each of your topics you speak on should have a separate file for new ideas.

Always Use Real Stories, Don't Invent or Borrow Them

I am amazed by how much stealing goes on in the speaking business. People will hear someone else's story and tell it like it is their own. Don't do it.

Don't do it for two reasons. First, it's unprofessional and unethical. No further explanation needed.

Second, when people catch you, you look like a fool. I saw a speaker tell a story that I knew had happened to a friend of mine. Apparently, I wasn't the only one who noticed. As he got off the stage, someone came up to him and "busted" him. I have never seen a speaker's face get so red so quickly.

Personal Stories

Keep a file of interesting stories, things that happened or do happen to you personally. Don't start deciding in advance whether or not they will make good material for a speech or seminar. At this stage, you want to write down every personal story you can think of.

The key here is to have a place to write them down and catalog them. Again, don't worry about where you will be using them at this point; just capture the information.

I don't know how many great stories I have lost over the years before I started this system, but I know the number is significant.

Start right now by going through your mind and writing down anything you can think of that comes to mind.

Storytelling

Every great speaker needs to know how to tell stories. Stories will help bring your content to life. Stories will frequently serve as anchors for your content points.

The only way to get good at telling stories is through practice. Before practicing, you need to watch other speakers who tell stories and emulate the ones who you think do the best job.

There are a number of speakers in the industry who are known as good storytellers who, to me, come off as incredibly contrived and fake. I suppose I'm not your average audience member, but some of these storytellers reek of baloney when they speak.

The best way to not have this happen to you is to tell the story as if you were telling it to a friend. Make sure the story is your own and you haven't "lifted" it from someone else.

Just like it is with comedians, there is an incredible amount of "borrowing" of material that goes on with speakers. You can borrow quotes and statistics, but don't borrow personal stories. It will come off as fake in the end.

There are some people out there who give storytelling workshops. I've never been to any of them. If you feel like you need help in this area, you may want to go to one. Never sign up for one of these unless they offer a money back guarantee.

I have two techniques I always use in my stories. First, I let the audience get a little ahead of me in the story, letting them think they know where I am going. Then I surprise them with something completely opposite than what they expected.

Using Fiction and Movies

I think that reading good books and watching great movies will give you some good ideas about how to design and deliver your speeches and seminars.

The two main things you can learn from these two literary forms are how to create great openings and closings.

If you want to see a great opening, go rent the movie, "The French Connection." This or any of the good Bond movies catapults you into the action immediately. Many speakers, like many movies (and books) take a while to get going. As a reader, I will put a book down that doesn't grab me from the very beginning.

Although my literary friends find this reaction appalling, I think it's 100% analogous to your audiences. If you don't grab them from the start, they will turn off. Rarely will you have the chance to get them back. Don't lose them.

Statistics

Keep a file with statistics, any and all statistics that catch your eye. Keep a pen and paper handy while watching TV. You never know when 20-20 will come up with a very useable statistic. Don't trust yourself to remember the quote. Write it down immediately. Worry about where you will use them later.

Using Quotations

Many speakers use quotations. The key is to use them where it makes sense and not to overuse them. A large percentage of speakers I see seem to have the need to include a quote every 15 minutes whether it's appropriate or not.

The key to using quotes effectively is to start collecting them whenever and wherever you can find them. Some speakers I know then put them on their computers by category. Good idea. This way you can refer to that particular section wherever you are.

When you find an interesting quote, write it down. Keep a pen and paper handy near your TV, just in case you luck out and get something productive from the "idiot box." People look down on watching television. I don't! I think that people who attend your events watch a lot of television. If you want your speeches to have relevant examples, you have to use examples they can relate to.

Keep these quotes and worry about when and where you are going to use them later.

Quote books are fine, but they tend to give you the standard kinds of quotes by the standard kinds of people. BORING! I like the idea of finding and using quotes that are more obscure. Your audiences will appreciate these kinds of quotes as well.

Another great way to use quotes is to get them from various prominent individuals in the company you are speaking to or from an industry expert that everyone would be familiar with.

People Love Lists

Except for the ten commandments, which had a rough review when first released, people love lists. You can't turn on the news without hearing about another list of some sort or another, best dressed, worst dressed, top ten this, top twenty that.

I use lists in my seminars whenever appropriate. I tell people in my self storage seminars about the top seven "return on marketing dollar" items.

I give speakers at my speaking seminars the five deadly sins you can't commit when doing a keynote. The 11 Commandments of Customer Service is the title of one of my keynotes on customer service.

And the list goes on. People love lists. Find ways in which you can incorporate your lists into your speeches and seminars. Following this strategy will also get you more press coverage.

Take Home Items

There is a speaker I know named Larry Winget who does a speech where he hands out a silver bullet to everyone in his audience. It is very effective. He uses it to prove a point and people always keep the bullet. I did. He shows people exactly what they should do with the bullet and where to keep it.

This kind of a take home item can be very effective if not used strictly as a gimmick. In his case it made a lot of sense and did not seem contrived.

I have seen other speakers attempt this type of thing with precisely the opposite effect. If you have any doubts, email me and tell me what you're thinking of doing. I will give you my feedback.

Stimulate All the Senses

When you do seminars or speeches, try to appeal to all of your participants' senses. This means showing great visuals, using music and finding any and every way you can to appeal to your audience.

Using these techniques are effective when not done strictly to use them for effect. If you need everyone in your audience to taste something, then it may be appropriate to pass something out for everyone to try. If it is done only for show, and doesn't prove a very important point, leave it out.

True/False: Sit Down and Stand Up

Another way you can get physical movement into your presentations and do so for a good reason is the true-false, sit down and stand up routine.

This involves asking your audience members to stand up or to sit down based on questions you ask. If the answer is true, tell them to stand up and, if it's false, to stay seated.

This is a great way to get people to do something physical and it will also accomplish a real purpose: to give you and the group an answer to a specific question.

Physical Movement

During your seminar you need to get people up and moving around. Occasionally, you will find a seminar leader or speaker who understands the need for movement, but gets people up and moving around with no specific purpose. This doesn't work. If you get people up and moving around, it must be purposeful.

An example of how to use this concept effectively is to get people to move to different corners of the room in response to a question. If you ask a multiple choice question, you can assign a different corner as representing each response category. When people go to a specific corner it will give everyone the results of your questions and do so in a way that makes the responses easy to visualize.

Physical movement is great to break up the seminar, but it always must have a purpose.

Physical Illustrations

Physically illustrating a point during a speech or seminar can be very effective. If appropriate, I encourage you to use this device.

I remember Lou Heckler (one of my favorites) lying down to illustrate a point of how long a particular long jumper had jumped. It was very relevant to his speech and worked very well within his context. With any "trick" like this, use them sparingly and only when it really makes sense. Don't just throw something in because you think it would be fun.

Visual Aids

Having fancy visual aids are no guarantee that people will love your presentations. I think you should mix your media at the seminar. It will help to keep peoples' attention.

By this I mean using the overhead sometimes, occasionally throwing in a video, then using a group exercise, then using a flip chart. The key here is to reduce the boredom factor. Keep things moving.

Many speakers make use of a lot of visual aids. A few years back, this consisted of slides and overheads. Those days are gone. Now, virtually everything is on computer with a Powerpoint presentation.

Let me lead this off by saying that you can't take an average speaker and improve them with great visuals. In fact, a weak speaker will look even weaker when they have an impressive visual presentation. The reason? People will pay more attention to the visuals than they do to the speaker.

Some Key Elements

Never use more than six lines of text and never more than six words on each line. This is a hard and fast rule you should never violate.

Don't overdo your use of colors. Use colors for dramatic effect, but don't make colors what people concentrate on with your visuals. Content should still be king.

Avoid using more than one or two typestyles; it will get confusing if you violate this rule. Also, use upper and lower case type as opposed to just upper case. It is very tough to read things when they are in upper case only.

In addition to whatever high tech devices you want to use for displaying your visual aids, I would always keep the trusty overhead projector around. This is for a few different reasons. First, I always carry back-ups of all my computer presentations in a hard copy form. This way, if the computer goes on the fritz, I won't be left empty handed.

I also like having an overhead around to do some writing "on the fly" in answer to an audience member's question that demands a written response.

You will also be able to use the concept of incorporating a local news story if you have an overhead projector. I spoke about this earlier.

Additionally, make sure that any visual is easy to read from the furthest point back in the auditorium.

Each visual should also communicate a single idea. They should also be relevant, interesting, simple and accurate.

Props

Props can be a great addition to your speech or seminar if they don't look contrived or gimmicky.

A prop should never be thrown in just for effect. It must have a purpose and be used to enhance and illuminate a content point. Speakers who throw in some random prop just to use them are foolish. It will make no sense and confuse your audience.

Some speakers use magic tricks. These are fine to use as long as the same principles are applied to them as well.

How do you find props or magic tricks? I find them being used in other contexts other than speaking and adapt and adopt them for use in my presentations. Use too many of them and you risk looking like the comedian Gallagher.

Using Music in Your Presentations

Music can certainly enhance your speech or seminar if used correctly. I encourage you to find a way to stimulate all your audiences' senses when speaking.

Here's the problem. Using copyrighted music without the appropriate permission is illegal and can cause you some huge problems. If you have your own original music, you're fine, either that or copyright free music.

There has been some discussion lately among other speakers I know about how much music you can use without needing permission. My suggestion is to err on the side of safety. Don't do it. I have seen some people get some pretty hefty fines.

The other discussion was whether or not you could use music if you were doing a not-for-profit event. Again, be careful and ask permission before going ahead with it.

How do you get permission? Call the local division of ASCAP in your area. They will give you all the information necessary. Find them by going to ascap.com. Don't be surprised if the fees are pretty steep. I was amazed at what they wanted to charge me for very limited use of one song. The net result? I found another way of doing things to avoid having to use that specific piece.

Do they really prosecute people for this kind of violation? Not often, but do you want to risk it? I don't.

Handling Hecklers

You will, on occasion, get people who heckle you as a speake, some in very direct ways and others in more indirect ways.

The chances of this happening at an internal corporate or association event are low. People are generally concerned that this behavior will get back to their superiors and make them look bad.

The most likely events where you will get hecklers are at large seminar events where people have been forced to go by their boss. When they get to the event, many aren't open to the idea of learning and are looking for a way to have fun at your expense.

You can never win a battle when you confront the heckler head on. I have tried it. It doesn't work.

Your best reaction is contingent upon what type of heckler you encounter.

One way is to pull the person aside at the break and ask for their help.

Another possibility is that you can ask them to give a presentation at some time towards the end of the day or the session so they have to spend their time preparing rather than bugging you.

You can also ask people in the audience for support. When someone is in the middle of some kind of negative behavior, ask the audience whether or not people would like for this person to continue or to move on. In every case, you will have the large majority of people shouting at the person to shut up.

People Who Look Like They Aren't Happy

You will be doing a seminar at some point in the future (or it may have happened to you already) and someone will look like they aren't interested. They will be looking out the window or in some other way appearing disinterested. You will get bothered by this fact. Maybe they aren't giving you eye contact, or maybe they are reading something unrelated to the seminar topic.

Don't spend your time trying to get this person to pay attention and do what you think they should be doing at the seminar.

This happened to me a number of years back when doing a big public seminar in Charlottesville, Virginia. There were three women in an audience of approximately 200 who I noticed early on in the session.

I spent the entire day trying to get their attention. The more I tried, the worse it got. I looked in their direction, and I walked over towards them to try to get them involved. Nothing helped. I got very frustrated.

The net result? My session suffered with the rest of the group. If people aren't interested, for whatever reason, don't try to get them to "love" you. It won't work and it won't help.

The only person's feeling and actions you have control over are your own. You can do your best as a speaker and that's it. Trying to do more will be a losing proposition.

Dealing with Stage Fright

It is certainly normal for you to have a certain amount of stage fright. If you don't have any stage fright when you speak, you will probably come off as uninspired.

In order to not have this fear overcome you there are a couple of key elements to remember.

First, you are most nervous when you first get started. To get through the first few minutes of your presentation, have your opening down cold. It should be memorized. When you deliver the information, however, it should not appear that way.

Second, make sure you do some meeting and greeting before your presentation gets started. This will make you feel as if you already have a certain number of friends out in the audience rooting for you to succeed.

Lastly, if you have a way tested that works, use it. This will loosen people up and get them on your side from the beginning.

This is not the time to test out any new "funny" material that hasn't been tried and tested. If you go for a laugh that doesn't work, you will be even more nervous than before.

Knowing When to Stop

Many speakers don't know when to stop.

In a loosely constructed presentation that isn't perfectly scripted, you may not have a specific point at which you have decided to stop. In my case, I usually have a few key stories I like to end with, but I may not always use them.

Let me give you an example. In a presentation I gave not long ago, I was able to ad-lib from something someone said in the audience.

It was getting near the end of my allotted time and I got a huge round of applause. On the spot, I made the decision to stop right there. The net result? I looked like a genius, as if I had planned it. I walked off stage and people were still chuckling.

I learned this a long time ago from friends of mine who are comedians. Comedians are usually given a certain block of time, let's say 15 minutes. If they tell a joke that works incredibly well at the 13 minute mark and they have people roaring in the aisles, they look out into the audience and say: "Thank you, ladies and gentlemen, and good night."

All comedians love to get through all of their material. Comedians feel ripped off if they are given 15 minutes but only use 13. But if they have really "killed" with a particular joke or ad-lib, they know it's time to get off the stage and leave people with that happy feeling inside about their performance.

As a speaker, you need to be able to do the same. As long as you have gotten through your content points, end when your audience tells you to.

Never End Late

One of the cardinal rules of speaking in either the speaking or seminar business is to end on time. This can sometimes be difficult.

Many times you are told that you will have 50 minutes for your presentation. When you get up to speak, your host or hostess will whisper in your ear that all you have is 35 minutes.

Going over your allotted time in this situation is strictly unacceptable. Why? Because you have been told that you have to cut it down. Many speakers somehow feel it IS acceptable to end late when they are not told of any particular changes that have been made to the program schedule. This is extremely unprofessional and will make you look very bad.

In order to never end late you have to have material that you can leave out if absolutely necessary. You will have an approximate idea of how long your various modules will take. Eventually you will get very good at knowing how long each module will take. Cutting a module or two and adjusting one or two others will allow you to cut your time and keep your presentation more or less intact.

When you have an event where your host cuts your time, they know that this causes most speakers a great deal of "agita" and will be even more impressed if you can both pull it off and do so without bitching and moaning.

With your own self-sponsored events, you will get your audience members annoyed at you when you don't finish on time. This will affect both your evaluations and your product sales. So, learn how to adjust to changing times and never end late!

You Are Not Your Audience

I mentioned it just briefly early on in the book, but if you think that people think like you, you may or may not be right. In my case, I find that I am usually wrong on this one.

Why? This is because of the fact that your participants may be very different than you in terms of their demographics. It's possible that is not the case. But if it is true, you need to know and understand what your group consists of and what they like and don't like. Don't assume that you know how they think. You may be dead wrong. Research is the only way to find out.

Exceed Audience Expectations

Many people come to seminars and don't expect much. They have been to plenty before and none of them were really all that good.

I like to have people leave my seminars and speeches feeling like they have gotten a ton of information and content. I'm even more excited when someone tells me it was the best seminar they have ever attended. Occasionally, people will tell you that you've changed their lives. This is pretty powerful stuff.

It's nice to work doing something where you can both make a lot of money and have this kind of impact on people. I encourage you to work hard enough at your speeches and seminars to get these types of reactions. Once you hear it, you'll be sold.

What About Low Attendance?

What should you do when only five people show up for some kind of an event that you are doing? Most speakers will act like this has never happened to them. Let me warn you in advance — IT WILL!

Let me illustrate with a story. About 12 years ago I gave a program at the Learning Annex in New York City. Only five people showed up. Most speakers (myself included) like to speak to big groups. It makes us feel a lot more important. You are also computing how much money you will be making in product sales.

As there were only five people there, the tendency of most speakers would be to give a less than enthusiastic performance, and perhaps even bitch about the number of people who were (or weren't) there.

I resisted the temptation. I delivered the information as if the room were full. I did sit down while delivering the information (which was appropriate in a group of this size), but I was careful to give them their money's worth in terms of both style and substance.

What happened? The same thing that may happen to you one day, so listen carefully. One of the ladies in attendance was the editor of a large and nationally known publication. She didn't let me in on this at the time. When she called me later to have me come in and do some training work for the people at her magazine, that is when I found out.

The moral of this story? Even if you have five people in the room, give your presentation at the same level of quality. First, you never know who is in your audience and second, the participants shouldn't suffer because there are very few in attendance. They paid THEIR money and they deserve the same level of performance as if the room had been packed.

Using Hard Data to "Sell" Your Results

When you give information to people in your audience, make sure you can back it up with specifics and sources. I have to admit that I have been guilty of making this mistake myself, but I always audit my work to sort out the problem areas.

How many times have you heard a speaker get up and talk about an issue and say something like, "Research shows us that ...". The question I always ask when I hear this line is, What research? Where did you get it? Is the source biased?

When you give people information that may challenge their existing ideas and beliefs, make sure tell them where you got the information and why the source should be believed.

I like to do a certain limited amount of my own research. It is always easier to forcefully present your data when it was accumulated on your own. In order to keep the data credible, make sure to tell people how you collected it.

Be Easy to Do Business With

You would think that I shouldn't even have to mention this. I wish I didn't have to, but I do. I know from my own experience that there are certain speakers and seminar leaders that are jerks and impossible to deal with.

Unless you don't care about the future of your business, you need to treat people well, from the moment they call until you sell them your consulting services. Make a mistake at any point in the process and risk alienating people who could put money in your pocket.

There will be the occasional jerk where you're are probably better off going somewhere else to do business, but that is very infrequent.

Treat people as well as you possibly can, they pay your rent.

Treat Everyone with Equal Respect

I was just visited by a very close friend here in New York last night while writing this particular section of the book. He is the manager of a very nice, celebrity frequented, restaurant.

The owner of the restaurant is a brilliant promoter and publicity hound. I say this with a lot of admiration. His problem is this. When you walk into his restaurant and he is at the bar, he will look to see who you are. If you aren't a celebrity or someone who can ostensibly help the man's business, he will look at you briefly and then quickly look away and ignore you.

You should see the difference when someone "important" walks through his doors. His face immediately lights up and he quickly walks toward them to welcome them through the door.

Remember this when you do your seminars and speeches. Don't treat anyone differently just because they are a well know entity. Remember, everyone starts as less than a celebrity, so you never know if you are meeting someone who will eventually be a big shot.

You Can't Please Everyone

You can't make everyone happy. This is true in the seminar business as in any other business. Hopefully you will make most people happy. If not, you need to look at your content and style.

No matter how good you are, you will have nay-sayers. Don't let it bother you. Remember, some people don't like the Beatles. How can you complain?

Thank You Notes

Send thank you notes to both your hosts at every event that you speak at and to bureau salespeople if they were responsible for you getting the work. Do this and you will be doing just what your mother told you (or should have told you) to do. It works in this context as well. Your chances of getting asked back will be dramatically increased.

I would recommend that you use a very simple handwritten note. Don't spend big money on fancy stationery. It is more important that you send a note every time someone deserves to be thanked.

Mixing Business and Pleasure

As a speaker at any event you become a mini-celebrity for a period of time. Along with this temporary celebrity status comes all of the attendant nonsense.

Let me give you an example to illustrate. I was once doing a presentation in Australia. After the event, I took a walk with one of the female participants. Forgive me, I am a heterosexual male. This walk created an international incident. There were all kinds of suggestions and innuendos. No matter what I did, it made no difference. My name had been tarnished.

Here is what I learned and what I will pass along to you as a result of this experience. Don't ever mix business with pleasure as a speaker. Just picture the National Enquirer ready to pounce on any indiscretion, no matter how innocent or minor, and blow it up to 100 times its size.

Act as if you are Truman in the movie "The Truman Show" while you are speaking at any event. Picture a camera following you around from the moment you step off the plane in the city you are going to be speaking. As in the movie, picture this camera recording everything you do, 24 hours a day.

Remember this and act accordingly.

Bureaus and More

Speakers Bureaus

Speakers bureaus serve as non-exclusive agents for speakers. There are a lot of them out there. Some are specialists in certain areas and others are generalists.

To get a list of bureaus, contact IGAB. They can be found at www.igab.org, The International Group of Agents and Bureaus (listed in the resource section). Be careful. They frequently don't have an updated list with the correct information. Make sure that they guarantee you (in writing) that you will get less than 5% returns on any mailer. If they don't, don't buy it.

Speakers bureaus take anywhere between 20% and 30% of the speaker's fee. It sounds like a lot of money and in my mind it is. However, another way to look at things is this. They are one portion, and only one portion, of your marketing mix.

Treat them like another client. You may send out information to 20 or more bureaus. This same group may say that they are anxious and excited to work with you. After a year has gone by, you will see that you are only really working with 3 or 4 consistently. Don't be surprised or disappointed with these results.

Here's the major dilemma for a speaker. When you need the bureaus, they don't need you. After you have established yourself as a speaker, they will get calls for you and all they will do is call you up and get a huge chunk of your fee for just making a phone call or two. This, to me, is a royal rip-off.

Talk to the bureaus and they will give you a big song and dance about how much work they have to do and how much overhead they have. Baloney! For the most part, they are vastly overpaid in the majority of situations.

Will the Bureaus Work with You?

Speakers Bureaus will only work with those individuals who are fairly accomplished speakers. I'll define a fairly accomplished speaker as one who can generate at least $2,500 per speech. Speakers they work with must also have a good video "demo" tape. If you aren't yet at the point where you satisfy these two requirements, you are not yet ready for a speaker bureau.

So, Should You Work with Bureaus?

Here's how I see it. You definitely should work with them in the beginning, when you need them. After you get to be a known entity, that is when the bureaus are getting paid for very little work.

It is then that you have to make a choice. Either you have to work on getting your engagements strictly through your own means, or put up with (better yet, negotiate lower) and fees that they charge.

When you are in a position to work with bureaus, don't send out your information cold. You need to contact someone and explain who you are as well as what topics you speak on. Then ask them if they would be willing to look at your demo tape and other promotional information.

If they agree, send it to their attention directly. This way you will not end up on the bottom of a huge pile of speaker materials that bureaus receive daily. I have been in their offices and seen these piles, and they are huge. Don't get lost in this morass. Never send out information without calling first.

After you send the material, follow up to make sure it was received. Then ask the individual how long you should wait to call them back to see what the next step would be. Follow up with them based on their answer to that question.

Sleazy Bureaus

If you run across a bureau that asks you to pay some kind of up front fee to be considered, I would take a pass. Legitimate bureaus will not charge you to review your information.

Bureau Sales Representatives

Bureaus may have a number of different speakers who speak on your topic. In addition to being good, it doesn't hurt to schmooze the individual sales reps for the bureau. They are not immune from receiving perks from speakers. They will oftentimes give you a stronger recommendation than another speaker who speaks on the same topics simply because you treat them well.

Bureau Friendly Materials

Bureaus expect that you will send them what is referred to as "bureau friendly" materials. This is material that has contact information in them. In the days of the internet, clients can always find a way to contact you directly, but they still remain uptight about this matter.

If you are going to work with them, ask them what they need, and give them what they want. If not, you won't get any work from them as a group.

What About Spin-Off Business?

Leads that are generated from a speaking engagement belong to the bureaus that set up your original speech or seminar. If you steal a lead and it gets back to them you will be in pretty hot water. If you agree to work with bureaus, work within their rules.

This would include handing leads over to them and giving them a piece of your product sales at an event.

How I Really Feel About Speakers Bureaus

This is an area that will get me in big trouble when I tell you the truth, but here goes. Most speakers bureaus are a complete and total rip-off.

Here's how they work. They charge you anywhere from 20% - 30% of your total fee for taking or making a phone call and sending out some information.

I had a run-in with one well known name in the speaking business who now owns a speakers bureau. He told me my materials were not "bureau friendly" and that he wouldn't send my stuff out. How's that for a "trusting" relationship?

Now, don't get me wrong, there are speakers who will get a lead generated by a speakers bureau and STEAL it. But that happens very infrequently.

Another war story from a speakers bureau goes like this. I was good friends (or so I thought) with an individual who owned a speakers bureau.

I had just written a book and needed the person's help with a friendly quote. The answer? This individual was too busy. They could not find time in their busy schedule for me. That's what good friends are for, right?

Work with bureaus in the beginning, but use my suggestions and be able to be "Bureau Free" as quickly as possible. They overprice their services for the work they do.

Speaker Showcases

Many speakers bureaus put on something they call showcases. This is where a group of speakers are given a limited time (usually 10 - 15 minutes) to speak for a group of meeting planners who book speakers. They speak one after the other in rapid succession.

The goal is for the meeting planners to get a first hand look at some of the speakers and see how they really do with a live audience. Demo tapes and other materials have fooled many a meeting planner in the past and this is a way to see how the speaker looks in person.

The bureau usually puts up somewhere between 10 and 20 speakers for the group. By the end of this ordeal (which it usually is for both speakers and meeting planners alike,) everyone is bleary-eyed. Unless a meeting planner has been taking very good notes, it may be difficult to remember which speaker said what.

If you do a showcase, never be the first in the morning or the last two or three of the day. If you are asked to take this position on the program, either ask for a serious reduction of the price or don't go at all. The latter is probably the better recommendation.

Your best slot is to be in the morning but before lunch. That way the meeting planners can see you and you can schmooze them over lunch. The lunch is usually held in a separate room where speakers and meeting planners can interact.

Bureau fees for these events will run somewhere between $500 and $1,000. My personal feeling is that the bureau should take this as an additional surcharge off of any speaking engagement that you land as a result of showing up at the event.

But as you can probably imagine, bureaus use these events to not only generate speaking engagements for their clients, but to turn a profit as well. Although this doesn't sit particularly well with me, it seems to be the way of the future.

I have only done two of these in my life. I had mixed feelings. I recall getting a speaking engagement or two out of them, but it still rubbed me the wrong way.

I also get the feeling that if you are asked by a bureau to appear in a showcase and you do go, they will tend to push you a little bit harder to their clients. This may or may not be true, but I have heard the same from a number of speakers.

Your key contacts at the bureaus aren't the bureau owners who many speakers try to cozy up to, but the bureau sales reps. They are your key to success. Schmooze them and you'll end up better off.

Best Time to be on a Program

When you are speaking at an event with multiple speakers, positioning is crucial. You will sometimes have the opportunity to give your input as to when you will appear on the program. There are certain times you definitely don't want to be speaking if you can avoid them.

With a program of any length, you do not want to be speaking on a Monday or Friday.

Whatever you do, don't give a presentation during a meal if you can help it. The next worst slot comes right after lunch where people are digesting that huge meal they just had.

If you can arrange it, mornings are better than afternoons. But, never first thing in the morning. Shoot for the second slot in the morning if you can get it.

If you have to speak in the afternoon, make sure you aren't the last speaker of the day, if you can avoid it.

My ideal time to speak is around 10 or 10:30 in the morning. Presumably, your audience has been up and awake for a while.

If you can pick your slot in a multi-day program, try not to be on either the first or the last day. Unless you can be the keynote speaker that kicks off the event. This is considered to be the most desirable speaking slot. They reserve this spot for their biggest name speaker.

It's also a good idea to find out who you will follow. I would never want to follow Colin Powell. I'm a pretty good speaker, but it's tough to follow a guy who helped win the Gulf War.

Dealing with Meeting Planners

Meeting planners are the people who coordinate many of the meetings you will be speaking at. They are the folks who will collect the information on the various speakers. Although they will have input on who their organization uses as a speaker, they are rarely the sole decision makers.

They accumulate the various speakers' materials, screen them, and then show them to a committee that has been assigned the task of selecting the speaker or speakers. For the meeting planner, this can be a dangerous job.

If they book a speaker who turns out to be a dud, they are in deep "doo-doo." It will look like they screwed up the meeting, that they blew it. The net result is that most meeting planners like to make decisions on speakers that are safe. This means sticking to someone who has a track record, and preferably one who has written a book on the topic. If the speaker does flop, they can always fall back with a line like, "How would I have known they weren't a great speaker, they wrote the book on XYZ."

As a speaker, you have to understand that most of the people who book meetings are not professional meeting planners. This is not their full time job. They have been "lucky" enough to handle the chore for this particular meeting. Most of them took this job reluctantly and are deathly afraid of what I described above. This being the case, you have to be prepared for mistakes being made; be tolerant. Remember, many meeting planners don't do the job full time.

Your goal is to make them look as good as possible. Do this and you will get a great letter of recommendation. Forget this and risk having them bad mouth you both internally and to anyone else that will listen to them.

You need to romance them. Treat them like you need them. Make them feel wanted. Coddle them.

They will ask you dumb questions. Don't be indignant. They will ask you the same questions over and over. Don't get annoyed.

Make their job easy and they will love you. Make their job difficult and they will never forget!

Generating In-House Seminars

In addition to public seminars you will also find that a certain number of people will want to bring you in to do an in-house seminar, which is tailored to their organization.

This is a very profitable business. Expenses are extremely low. Someone sees you doing your thing in a public seminar and they ask you to basically do the same thing for their internal employees.

Many speakers and seminar leaders will do a lot of outbound marketing to try to generate this type of business. I wouldn't recommend it. In-house business is much better and more profitably generated via indirect marketing.

Or perhaps they hear about you from someone else who had a great experience with you. Another possible way that you will get in-house work is from doing a lot of advertising in a specific market niche. They will see your advertising enough that when they need your expertise for an in-house seminar, they may just pick up the phone and call you.

Whichever way you get it, it produces some very nice, high margin business for you.

To make in-house seminars more likely, when speaking at public seminars make sure to put a space on the evaluations where you ask people if they are interested in having a program brought directly to their company. Also, the follow-up you do is essential in making this happen. Follow up quickly with anyone who expresses an interest. If you wait too long, they will lose their enthusiasm.

Your book or books that you write should also include information about the fact that you do these kinds of seminars. You will get a fair number of calls this way as well.

International Opportunities

There are speaking opportunities all over the world. As you follow the guidelines I have laid out here, you will inevitably get invited overseas to speak.

Although it sounds glamorous, speaking overseas is very tiring. It's exhausting to constantly be on airplanes.

Do it a few times if you need to get the "bug" out of your system.

If you are really intrigued by doing presentations internationally, let your speakers bureaus know that you are interested. Many people, like me, don't pursue these engagements actively, so your chances are probably pretty good once you establish yourself as a speaker.

Yes, you can then legitimately claim that you have spoken "in over 43 countries," as I heard one speaker say.

When I worked with CareerTrack, I did numerous overseas seminars and speeches. I have also done a number of them on my own.

My conclusion? Leave overseas travel for vacation. Not work!

Try it; my guess is you will come to a similar conclusion.

The Association Market

Many speakers aren't wild about speaking to the association market. They look at it as the low rent part of the speaking business. Most speakers would prefer to do work within the corporate environment. I couldn't disagree more forcefully.

When you speak for an association, it is true that they may not pay the big fees that corporate clients are willing to spend, but remember, fees for your speaking engagements are just one source of your income.

If you can customize some products. and they allow you to sell, you can make a lot more money than any corporate gig you will ever speak at.

People who belong to associations also work for corporations. Association speaking engagements become a showcase for corporate personnel who work elsewhere and may have a need for a speaker at a future event. If you do a good job, you will be showcasing your talents for a lot of people who may hire you to work at other corporate events.

My biggest paydays have been at association engagements. As I mentioned, I made over $50,000 in one hour and continue to have my biggest paydays from association gigs where I can sell products.

College Market

The college market for speakers is a specific niche in and of itself. The market is not particularly lucrative and product sales are rarely a possibility. They tend to book political speakers or those with controversial social topics.

The speakers are usually booked by a student committee. This means that finding and identifying the decision maker is difficult. In addition, the "key players" change every semester in most cases.

There is a way to showcase all of the individuals who book speakers. They convene on a regular basis and you can arrange to present at or attend this event.

If you are interested in working in the college market, my suggestion is to write a book that is either political in nature or is a topic that will appeal to college students.

If you have written a book on dating and relationships, that topic would be a perfect fit.

If your goal is the maximization of revenue, this is probably not the primary market you should pursue.

Working Cruise Ships as a Speaker

Many speakers love speaking on cruise ships. This enables them to get paid for taking a great vacation.

When you are booked on a cruise ship you have to do a certain number of presentations for the week. They give you free room and board and a fee for presenting. If you like cruises, this isn't a bad deal.

As you can probably imagine, you and a million other speakers want these gigs. The competition is tough.

Once again, the best way to get this type of business is through precise niche marketing. Let's say you are a speaker who specializes in investment related issues. There are a number of cruises that also target this same group of customers. You need to contact the promoters of these events and let them know that you would like to be considered.

Having written a book or numerous articles in the field will make your chances of getting selected much higher. You can also contact the cruise lines directly. Call the major cruise lines up and ask who is responsible for selecting their speakers. I would give you a name of a certain position, but it varies with each cruise company.

Once you contact that individual, send them your promotional material. Then follow up with a great postcard every month to keep your name and face in front of them. Do an occasional follow up call, but don't be a pest.

Letters from Government Officials

It is fairly easy to get a letter of commendation from a variety of government officials. Public officials are required by law to respond to any correspondence from their constituents. This makes it easy for you to get letters from numerous key and impressive public officials. On their official letterhead!

In your promotional material why not have a letter from your hometown mayor, your senator and congressman, and even the president? All you have to do is write to them and tell them why you should receive a letter of commendation. In many cases they will take your letter and repeat back to you what you told them, almost verbatim.

Take these letters and include them in any and all promotional material that you send out.

Strategic Volunteering

A great way to get seen by the right people in your community is to volunteer. Volunteer for causes that you have a genuine interest in, but also use these occasions to showcase your talents and abilities to others who are involved in the group.

Many times, as part of your volunteer efforts, you will be asked to make a short speech or introduce someone. This is a mini-showcase for you. Take advantage of this opportunity.

When you give any speech or introduction to this group, make sure to include the following line just once during your opportunity to speak. In the course of your speaking say, "In a recent speech/seminar that I gave to XYZ corporation I found that . . . "

Never do this more than once. If you do, it will look very much like you're giving a sales pitch. One mention, on the other hand, is completely acceptable.

There is a very strong probability that you will impress someone in the audience who has a company that needs you as a speaker or seminar leader.

Getting Yourself an Award

They give out awards for almost everything! How many times have you been going through a newspaper or magazine and seen someone who was just awarded the "ABC Award" for basket weaving professionalism? Don't laugh, they probably have one!

How did they get this award? They asked for an application and applied to receive this award. You need to do the same. You will obviously want to focus on those awards that would be advantageous to your speaking and consulting business.

Many of the awards that are given out aren't just given to one person but to many, so your chances of receiving one are dramatically increased.

Filling out the award application may take a little time, but it is well worth it. Just wait until you get your first and you'll know what I mean. Now get on it!

Generating Repeat Business

Getting repeat business is a lot easier than going out hunting for new business. You have all heard the statistic, (I have no idea where it comes from), that it costs five times as much to get a new customer than it is does to keep an existing one.

Getting repeat business as a speaker consists of three primary components.

First, you have to be good. This means delivering highly relevant and useable content in a highly entertaining manner.

Second, you have to be well liked by your hosts. Don't confuse this with the first item. You can definitely give a great speech with useable content and have people not like you.

The way to do this is to be a great guest. If you behave like a prima donna, no matter how talented a speaker you are, you will not be invited back.

I have heard stories from clients about how poorly some speakers behave. They make ridiculous demands. They behave like rock stars. This is insane!

The best example of this kind of behavior comes from a video that I was doing a few years back. I had hired a number of New York actors. One of the actors was a veteran with over 20 years of experience, some of that ON BROADWAY.

The other actors were relatively young and inexperienced. One of them had to be sent home early. She was acting like a "diva."

This guy who was such a prince to work with is Ed Steele. He volunteered to do anything. Nothing was beneath him. He went out in the morning and got everyone coffee and donuts.

This is the same guy who toured with Julie Harris for many months in "Driving Miss Daisy." This is the kind of behavior that gets you invited back as an actor. It is the same kind of behavior that will get you invited back as a speaker.

Be easy to deal with. Offer to help doing anything. Don't put yourself on a pedestal. People will love you for being a "regular" person. Think of the great reputation Tom Hanks has in the acting community. You have to be perceived in the same manner as a speaker if you want to get tons of repeat business.

Two key additional reasons why you want to be perceived as easy to work with. First, people who are at one organization frequently move and go to another organization. They may use you again when they go to the next company. Another is that all the people in this business talk. If their word is good, it will get out. If it's bad, it will get out even faster.

Finally, the last thing you have to do to generate repeat business is follow-up. Once someone has used you as a speaker, keep in touch with them a minimum of four to six times a year.

Generating Referrals
as a Speaker

Referrals are the best way to get speaking engagements. There is very little hard sell necessary when you come highly recommended.

The best way to generate a ton of referrals is to do a great job of speaking.

Additionally, referrals come as a result of asking for both your participants and those who booked you.

Let the audience know somewhere towards the end of your presentation that you welcome them referring you. Don't oversell it, but let them know you want them. Remember, people in your audiences have lots of contacts. Take advantage of this fact.

There is no one more helpful than someone who has just heard you speak and likes you.

Getting those who booked you to refer you requires a different tact. I actually put a referral clause in my contract. My contract states that if the organization or association is happy with my presentation, they will give me at least two names of others who I may be able to talk to.

Before a client has signed a contract, I have occasionally had them ask me about this clause in the contract. I tell them that if they are happy, I do expect them to give me a few names.

You should do the same.

The Value of Handwritten Notes

Handwritten notes are a great way to keep in touch with both past and future clients. Since everything in our society is computer generated these days, you need to personalize your message. The best way I have found to do this is with handwritten notes.

Get some personalized stationery as well as a selection of cards. Some of them may be funny if that's your style.

When you follow up with people, do so this way. People are so inundated with automated messages of all kinds that the hand-written note creates an instant differentiation between you and other speakers.

Unusual Marketing Methods

I wanted to give you a few highly unusual but effective means of marketing your speaking business.

These are totally non-traditional methods of marketing. Use these as additional clever ideas that you can try. I am not suggesting you use these as a substitute for your traditional marketing techniques.

Whenever I am on a plane, I make sure to leave copies of my one page fact sheet in the seat pocket in front of me. I also put an additional one in the center of the magazine. Before leaving them in there, I always write a little note at the top that says, "This guy was great!" and then sign a made up name like "Jay" right below this note.

I have no data as to how many speaking engagements I have generated this way, but the cost is so low I figure it can't hurt.

If you are sitting up in first class, you may want to leave one of your demo tapes, hoping some big shot corporate executive will find it.

Although I'm not a Black Tie kind of a guy, I would suggest you occasionally shell out and go to these charity events.

I am a member of the Admirals club. This is the airline club owned by American Airlines. I suggest you join at least one of these clubs. They not only give you a great place to sit, relax and work during flights, but they offer excellent networking opportunities.

The demographics are perfect. A lot of mid to upper level corporate executives can be found in these clubs. Try to use your brilliant people skills to schmooze the people you meet in the clubs, and you will end up with a ton of great leads.

I remember a speaker talking about how he would go around to places with copies of his 8"x10" black and white glossy photos. He would walk into various stores and tell them he was a famous speaker. He would then volunteer to sign a picture and give it to them if they would put it up in the window. Clever!

Advertising

A lot of speakers waste a lot of money on advertising. I have done it myself. Please, please, please, don't make this same mistake. If you do any advertising at all, it should be done within one of your niche markets. And you should only do direct response advertising.

Here's a story to help you understand this. I was solicited one year to put an ad in a major associations handbook. Specifically, it was in the ASAE (American Society of Association Executives) book.

I spent $850 and it pulled one bogus call. Don't get conned into any advertising that can't be tracked.

Naturally the salesperson told me I would get deluged with calls. The net result? Just what I described. I'm pretty good at creating effective advertising so I don't blame myself. I put the blame squarely on the publication.

So, buyer/speaker beware. Don't do any advertising in any of these general publications. And again, feel free to email me a question on this point. I don't want to see you get taken by any slick talking salesperson.

So if you do want to advertise, do it in trade magazines in those niche markets that you have cultivated sufficiently to have their readers know who you are. Do this and your response rates will be much higher.

Infomercials

My experience with infomercials is instructive to all speakers who are thinking of how they can get rich using this selling methodology. I put one of the first infomercials on the air in the mid 1980's. To this day, I have clients I work with who have infomercials as one of their means of marketing.

The reason for a speaker's interest in this medium has been generated almost entirely because of Anthony Robbins' success selling his products via infomercial. In addition to making a lot of money selling products, he dramatically increased his profile as a speaker. This served to increase his demand as a speaker. The increase in demand translated into higher fees.

Every speaker I know who is looking to make big bucks and maintain a high profile sees infomercials as the way to go. Good idea if you have the right topic and the right TV presence to pull this off. Unfortunately, it very seldom is the case.

First, you must have a topic that has universal appeal. In Tony's case, he was dealing with a product that EVERYONE could potentially benefit from.

FREE SPEAKING TIPS:

To receive regular tips on how to start and build a successful speaking business send an email to:

tips@professionalspeakingsuccess.com.

Since I'm recommending that you niche yourself, it makes it tough, although some of your niches can be pretty large.

One of my books that will be out shortly is called: "The Home Based Business Marketing Success Manual." This is a huge niche. There are close to 40 million home-based business owners. It might be worth my testing an infomercial in this area because the size of the niche is so large. The problem is that it is still not an EVERYONE product like Tony sells.

The other problem is the huge number of dollars necessary for testing a concept like this.

You have two major costs to consider. First is the cost of producing the show. Second is the cost of the time on the stations where the show will air.

I produced an infomercial back in 1985 to market a lot of my products that had to do with starting and building your own consulting business. It included a book and a number of audio tape programs.

I was lucky in that my ex-partner knew about television production. This allowed us to put the show together for much less than anyone could have and we still produced a quality show. Our total cost for everything to put on a half hour and a one hour show "in the can" was under $3,000. Today it would cost you ten times that to even come close.

Next, I had to purchase time. Since this was a general topic with a financial bent to it (or so I thought), I went to what was then called FNN, Financial News Network. It has since been acquired by CNN. They would only sell me a minimum of five half-hour time segments.

Those five slots cost me around $15,000. That money was due in advance. GULP!

I wrote the check and imagined myself retired in the Bahamas with the huge flood of orders that would roll in as a result.

I had set up in Utah to handle the flood of orders that I would receive.

The night after the first show ran, I called the 800 number service to find out just how big a house in the Bahamas I would be living in. I gave them the code number to check the amount of orders that had been received from the night before. The operator got back on the phone and said, "No orders yet." I told them that was impossible and that they had checked the wrong box. I told her to check again. Same answer. YIKES!

I immediately called my media rep and told them to pull the remaining four half-hours we had bought. He got back to me 20 minutes later to say that it wasn't possible.

After all the shows had run, I had gotten 32 orders. Each one for $99 each. I had lost a whole lot of money.

Learn from my mistakes. Don't go out to the mass market until you learn how to target a niche. With all of the cable stations available, you now have a lot of options. Also, test in a very small market first before you roll out. This will save you a lot of money and aggravation.

Lastly, before you think about doing one, contact me to have a very serious discussion of the important issues you need to consider.

Doing Your Own Events

Doing Your Own Seminars

The goal of every seminar of mine is to maximize revenue. I assume your goal is the same. I am not looking only for short term revenue. I am looking to maximize total revenue both now and in the future.

Revenue is derived from three primary sources: Seminar registration, product sales and consulting business.

To be successful in the seminar business, you have to realize that there are four steps. First, you have to promote the seminar and get people in the room. Next, you have to give a great seminar. Then you have to get people to spend money with you at the seminar itself. Then you have to get them to come back to other seminars and events you have. Then you have to get them to buy more from you. Then you have to get them to use you as a consultant and to tell everyone else about you.

So now let's get started.

Public Seminars

Giving public seminars is how I got started as a speaker. It is the riskiest way I know to make a living. Promoting your own seminars is a scary business. You are responsible for every aspect of the event both administratively and financially.

As a a consultant, I also like the idea that it is the only way you can get people to pay to be prospects.

On the positive side, you are the master of your own destiny. No committees to decide whether or not they will let you speak.

When done correctly, marketing and promoting your own public seminars can be very lucrative. I have a complete six cassette program (listed on the order sheet in the back) that goes into every specific detail of the process. I am also finishing up a book on marketing seminars and workshops. Check the web site fredgleeck.com for details.

Seminars are usually promoted through two primary means, newspaper and direct mail. There are some people who promote using radio and TV, but they are usually people with big budgets like the real estate "gurus."

Some people are also trying to promote seminars on the web. The most effective way to do this is by using your in-house email list.

Remember the Public Seminar formula. TR = SR + PS + CB. Total revenue is equal to seminar registration, plus product sales, plus consulting business.

Depending on the size of the group and your product sales ability, you may be willing to just break even on the seminar registration dollars and then make a small bundle on product sales.

Over the years, a lot of research has been done and numbers have been kept regarding which days and which months pull the best registration numbers. There are two groups to consider when you do your own seminars: those who pay for the seminars themselves, and those where their organization or company pays for the seminar.

One Step vs. Two Step Seminar Promotion

There are two basic ways to promote seminars. First would be to create ads and other promotional devices which ask people to call and register for the seminar itself. This is called the one step system.

The two step promotional system asks people to come to a free hour or hour and a half mini seminar. It is really a disguised sales pitch. This method of promoting was popularized by the real estate gurus who got people into a room for 90 minutes and then sold them on the idea of coming to a full weekend seminar where they could supposedly make millions.

Best Days of the Week When the Attendee Pays
Saturday, Monday, Tuesday, Wednesday, Thursday, Friday, Sunday

Best Days of the Week When the Company Pays
Thursday, Wednesday, Tuesday, Friday, Saturday, Monday, Sunday

Best Months to do Seminars When Attendee Pays
January, October, September, March, June, April, February, November, May, July, December, August

Best Months for Seminars When Company Pays
March, October, April, November, September, February, January, June, May, August, July, December

All of these best months and days assume you are doing something that is not completely counter-cyclical in nature. That would mean that a boating seminar may work very well in July. But for the most part, follow this list.

The Public Seminar Formula

The formula you must understand before any serious discussion of seminars is TR = SR + PS + CB. Total revenue equals seminar registration plus product sales plus consulting business.

Understanding this formula is the difference between profit and loss in many cases. The uninformed observer will sometimes conclude you are not making any money when they show up at the hotel where you are giving seminars and count the number of people who come through your doors.

Those who think that the number of registrants is all there is are not computing the two additional factors that are so crucial to your long term success: the sale of products and the future consulting business that will inevitably result from the seminar. Registration dollars come in immediately. Product sales registrations come in almost immediately. Actually, if you market your products correctly, orders should come in for the foreseeable future.

Consulting business is something that comes in over a much longer period of time. It is also the item that can be your biggest revenue source. Not long ago someone attended a $297 seminar of mine.

They then bought the $777 package at the seminar. They then called up two months later and asked how much it would be to consult with me for three hours every month.

Initially, you won't truly understand how to compute your profitability because there will not be enough data on product sales and consulting. In time these numbers will become clear to you. Then and only then will you be able to compute seminar profitability and what total number of registrants it really takes to break even.

Seminar Titles

Coming up with a great title for your speech or seminar is critical to your success. It is one of the most, if not the most, critical element of your marketing unless you are a celebrity.

That being the case, you need to come up with great titles for any and all of your speeches and seminars.

Is there a formula? Yes and no. Some will tell you to use a formula: "How to blank, so that you can blank."

I would avoid clever titles that use a double entendre or some other play on words.

I have found the best way to create titles is to take your three or four best ideas and put them on a sheet of paper and show them to anyone and everyone and ask them which they like the most. Many time this has given me the best ideas.

Seminar Design

What should you include in the seminar? The first thing you need to do is to take your area of expertise and write out the top 25 or 30 major topics in the field that you will be focusing upon in the seminar.

What I suggest is you lay out each of the topics on index cards. If you think you have heard this before you're right. It's similar to what you might do when writing your book. Then brainstorm and lay your index cards on the ground. Fill up the index cards with at least four or five subheadings under each of your major topics which are on each card.

This will create your seminar outline almost instantly. Then decide upon the order.

Come up with a great introduction and a great conclusion. Go back and look at each of the major topics (each index card) and ask yourself some additional questions.

See if you can find sections where some of your quotes, stories, statistics, or props can be used effectively. Don't put them in unless appropriate, but do use them where they are.

Before You Choose a Seminar Date

This is a mistake I made the second year I started doing seminars. I decided to do a seminar on the last weekend in January. Not being a big football fan, I didn't realize this was Superbowl weekend. Attendance was much lower than I would have liked.

Before you decide on a firm date for your seminar, here are some important things to consider.

Check to make sure that the date you choose is not a vacation day for your target market group.

Another mistake is booking a seminar on a holiday. Look at the calendar carefully before you choose your date.

Religious holidays also need to be considered. Not just one religion, but all of the major religions that your target group may follow.

Sporting events, like my example above, are to be carefully considered before you do a seminar to an audience that is primarily male. Not to be sexist, but men are much more apt to miss seminars for a major sporting event.

When doing a seminar out of town, talk to their local chamber of commerce to make sure you are not in conflict with one their important local events.

When deciding on a seminar time, consider whether there will be a change in time as a result of daylight savings time. Mention this in your promotional material if it is on the day immediately after it is either withdrawn or put into place.

I made a big mistake in Tampa, Florida, one time when I told people to go the Airport Marriott Hotel. Little did I know there were two hotels that were considered to be the airport Marriotts. One was actually in the airport and the other was a mile or two away.

It's also not a great idea to give your seminar at the same time as the competition. Not that I mind competing, but it makes no sense to cut your registration numbers when you don't have to.

Seminar Locations

Many cities are perfect for holding your seminars and speeches. Hotels are the obvious ones. Most often used is the hotel meeting room. But this is by no means the only choice.

As I am writing this section, I just went to a place here in New York City that holds a lot of "new age" seminars. It's called the Source of Life and is located right near the Empire State Building.

It is a great space for holding an entrepreneurial seminar, but the friend who I met there who trains lawyers found it unacceptable. He found it a little too casual.

You must judge your audience and determine what makes the most sense. Spend the least you can , but don't let it hurt your registration numbers.

Early Enrollment Incentives

You have got to give people some incentive to call when they find out about your seminar. In the example I gave about my first seminar on consulting, I gave people $10 off if they registered before the day of the seminar. This helped get people to sign up immediately.

Many seminar providers will give people a step stair discount based on how quickly they sign up. The example would be $175 before March 1st., $195 before March 21st., $225 thereafter.

This will help to smooth out the demand curve. It will make the registrations come in sooner. This will help reduce the drastic "heart attack curve." You will get your registrations at a much more even pace. Again, test this one.

My latest is to give the first 10 people who sign up a video worth $99. This seems to work, but it can be expensive.

The best item I have found to give out is a critique coupon. This is a small piece of paper that I value at $150. It allows people to send me any piece of promotional piece and I will critique it. This has high perceived value to the potential seminar attendee and low cost to you. So think about coming up with something that is inexpensive, yet has high perceived value.

Advertising Your Seminar

There are two primary means of advertising your seminars. One is through print ads in the newspaper and magazines, and the other is through direct mail.

In all three of these areas you need to make sure to include the same elements, so if you understand one, you understand them all.

Advertorial Look

When you advertise in either the newspaper or in trade publications, your goal is to make your ad look as much like an article as possible. Try to match the format of the publication in terms of typestyle and even the column size.

Many publications won't let you do an exact typestyle match because they are concerned that your ad will confuse their readers into thinking it is their editorial. The way that they get around this, in addition to asking you to change a few things, is by "slugging" your ad. This is when they take your ad and put the word "advertisement" at the top of it to let people know that it is paid advertising and not editorial copy.

Even when they do this, the ads still work better than making your ads look like advertising. Remember, most people skip the ads to read the articles. Why not use this fact to make it more likely that people will look at your ads?

Before you start spending any money on advertising your own seminars, start studying what other people are doing. Get on everyone's' list. Also, make sure to test small. Don't ever roll out a campaign until you know it works. Trust me, I have made this mistake.

When you get to the point where you think you are big enough to consider radio and TV advertising, you need to call me. This is much too sophisticated and risky for most speakers.

Newspaper Ads and Print Ads

I started my career in seminars by running space ads in newspapers. I was promoting a one day seminar on a Saturday. I would run ads the two Sundays before for the one day seminar on the following Saturday. Back in the early '80s I gave my first seminar on "How to Start and Build a Consulting Business in Your Own Field." I spent about $2000 on advertising and promotion.

I ended up netting $2000 on a Saturday. I was ecstatic! The problem is that back then I did not understand the front end/back end concept. I may have made $2000, but I lost a lot more money by not having a decent back end.

I no longer make those mistakes. Live and learn.

The beauty of the newspaper ad is that you can decide you want to do a seminar today and three weeks from now be doing a seminar. It shortens the lead time for you to do a seminar.

Naturally, this will only work with general seminar topics. These are topics where your potential attendees read newspapers to get their information.

Let me go through the components of an ad you would run in a newspaper from top to bottom.

HEADLINES

PRE HEAD

The pre-head is at the very top of the ad, usually over to the far left. In my consulting example, my pre-head was: "One Day Seminar Coming Soon to Your Area." The headline that followed was centered.

HEADLINE ITSELF

The headline is the most important element of your ad. A change in a headline can result in a doubling or tripling in response rates.

In the case of my consulting seminar it read, "How to Start and Build a Consulting Business." Underneath this line in smaller type, but still part of the headline, I put in parentheses, "(in your own field)."

The formula for your headline is to take your greatest benefit and combine it with your potential participants' greatest needs.

Spend the most time on your headline. This is more responsible for your success than anything else.

POST HEAD

The post head is where you elaborate on what the headline promises. In the case of the consulting seminar I might have put (although I didn't in this case) something like, "If you want to get out from under your corporate job and make twice as much money, this is the event for you."

I gave people an incentive for registering in advance. They paid $85 in advance or were charged $95 at the door.

TESTIMONIALS

In order to have the best results, you must have comments from others who have attended your seminars in your ads.

The heading to this section might be, "What others say about the seminar." In this section, you will want to give specific quotes by people who have attended your seminars in the past. Be very careful that you have these quotes on file and documented. It would be a crime to include a quote that people did not actually say.

In order to give these quotes the greatest weight and impact, make sure to include the name of the person who gave you the quote and the city and state they are from. Never just give the quote and put R.J., Omaha, Nebraska. People don't believe these quotes.

WHAT YOU WILL LEARN

This is the section where you have to show people why they should be willing to spend their time and money to come. Your descriptions here are the biggest and most benefit-oriented items you will cover at your seminar.

You give them a whole list of them. Your hope is that one of these elements will get someone to stop and decide to register. Many people tell me at seminars that they came just to hear the information from one bullet point I listed in the ad.

This section should be done in a bullet-point fashion. It should be clearly focused on benefits participants will receive and should be done using a certain number of lists. Remember, people love lists.

You will want to have the "5 things you must do to ... " along with "7 deadly sins to avoid when you ...". Don't create every bullet point using this technique, but at least a third of them can be done this way and be highly effective.

SEMINAR FEE

We have discussed the topic of pricing. It should be clear and understandable what your price for the event is and what they get for the fee. Does it include lunch? Then tell them. Does it include anything else? If so, say so. Do people get a discount if they register by a certain date? Let them know.

I like to give people a financial incentive for registering by a certain date. They might pay $175 by "x" date, but $195 at the door.

I also say that the first "x" number of people who register will get a copy of my book for free. Either that or I tell them that I will give them a free gift worth $150. This is usually a critique coupon which I hand out to everyone who attends, not just those who qualified.

Also, make sure and let people know what method of payment they can use. You want to accept anything you possibly can. The minimum would be Visa, Mastercard, American Express, checks and cash. When I use the word check, I always follow it with the words: "with credit card guarantee" after it.

UNABLE TO ATTEND

You need to have this section in there to generate tape sales for those who can't make it. There are some seminar promoters who will recommend that you not include this section. They say it will damage the sale of seminar seats. I completely disagree. I have been doing this for years and it has never hurt my sales.

My exact line is almost always, "Unable to attend? Call for a complete set of seminar materials with telephone consultation."

TAX DEDUCTIBILITY

Make sure to include a section that relates to the possibility of this event being tax deductible. Most people know this, but it doesn't hurt to remind them of this fact. I have even seen some seminar providers include the exact tax code section that covers this area.

ATTENDANCE LIMITED

We want to appear like this event will be very popular. Do everything in your power to create urgency. Tell them that only the first "x" number of people will be permitted to attend, with no exceptions.

Direct Mail

Direct mail is one of the primary means of promoting seminars. It is in many ways more efficient than using newspaper advertising. When using direct mail you will have much less waste.

You will be able to target the exact group of people you think would be your ideal prospects, the reason being that you can generally find a list that very closely matches the group you are trying to target.

The elements in your direct mail piece should be the same ones that you use in your newspaper ads. The difference is that you put it in letter form.

Clients frequently ask me how long a direct mail piece for a seminar should be. The answer is one that no one ever likes, as long as it needs to be to sell people on signing up for your event.

I will usually promote a seminar by first sending out a cheap post-card that encourages people to call a seminar hotline. This postcard is then followed up by a very long letter where I write comments in the margins.

Magazines

If you know your seminar dates way in advance, magazines may be an ideal vehicle for you to use. Closing dates on magazines for advertising are often 60 - 90 days in the future. The best thing about magazines, particularly trade magazines, is that they are often read cover to cover.

In addition to having a long shelf life, people usually keep them sitting around until the next publication arrives.

Trade Publications

If you are doing seminars in a niche market, chances are there are at least one or two trade publications you could choose to advertise in. Dollar for dollar these often provide the best return for your dollar.

The one essential guide you need for getting articles published in niche publications is the International Directory of Little Magazines and Small Presses. This publication will give you a complete list of all of the magazines out there.

I am not suggesting you buy this item. Just go to your local library and look through it.

Pricing

Pricing is an important piece of the seminar puzzle. The lower you price the seminar, the more people will attend. This axiom is true MOST of the time. It would follow that this will give you more opportunities to sell your products. Right? Maybe! When you price the seminar too low, you might get people who come into the room who can't afford to buy your products.

If you price the seminar too high, you won't have enough people who might buy your products. What's the answer? TEST!

In my tests of a number of my markets I have found the $297 price to be the right one for a one day seminar. Please don't take this number and assume this number will work for you. It may. It may not. TEST!

The way I determined the right price was from computing the total amount of dollars that come in from the seminar as a result of the given price. I found that at the $99 price point people didn't buy much product. They also were pains in the butt to deal with. Very little consulting business resulted. This was obviously not the right price.

I then tried $495. I got a lot less fewer people at the seminar. They didn't buy all that much product. Some of the people became consulting clients. Price optimization for me occurs at $297. It seems to give me the best of everything

Seminar Hotlines

I use hotlines to sell seminars. This is a separate line I set up that gives people a detailed description of what will be covered at the seminar. It concentrates on the benefits of attending the seminar and should have numerical specifics attached to each of the benefits, something like: "Three things you must do if ... ".

I set this up on a local line. I usually get away setting up residential lines. This costs less money. All you need to do is attach an answering machine to the line. Don't use voice mail. Why? You can't do up to a 25 minute outgoing message. Not that I do one that long, but you could if you wanted.

I use a digital answering machine with the capability of doing a long outgoing message. Whichever machine you use, make sure it is digital.

Prepare a script and read it into the machine. Ask some people to listen to the hotline message. Get their feedback. Make changes accordingly that you think make sense.

People usually respond positively because you are hearing the real live voice of the person who will be doing the seminar. Don't use a professional voice person to do this. It is imperative that whoever will be doing the seminar is the same person who records the hotline.

The postcard sucks them in and the voice message really sells them. The person who needs a further push will call in and request more information.

Postcard Mailers

The idea here is an inexpensive way to get people to your seminar. I usually use the seminar and combine it with at least one more detailed mailer which comes right after people get the postcard.

The purpose of the postcard is not to try to sell them on the seminar. That would be absurd. You don't have enough space to make that happen. The purpose of the postcard is to get them to call the storage hotline. Let the storage hotline sell the program for you. If you have an effective hotline, it will, at a minimum, provoke a call from people who want more information. You should be armed with a minimum eight page fax or email to close the person on registering.

My suggestion would be to try the following. First send a postcard at about five or six weeks before the date of the seminar. Then, a week later, send your longer direct mail piece, and a week after that follow up with another postcard. Make it different from the first postcard.

The postcard shouldn't try to sell them on the seminar itself. It should try to sell them on picking up the phone and calling a hotline number that will then sell them on the seminar. There isn't enough space on a small postcard to try to do a sales pitch.

There is, however, a good chance that you can sell people on the idea of picking up the phone and making a call. This isn't asking too much.

The timeline I have given you is for mailers that you send to people who will be within 250 miles of the seminar location. When people have to travel further, the customer should probably be given a little longer to respond. You may want to add two weeks. Your first postcard would then go out eight weeks before the seminar. Your direct mail piece would go out six or seven weeks before the date. The last postcard mailer would go out four to five weeks before the date of the seminar.

The major reason why you must give people some additional time is for planning and airfare purposes. People who must get on a plane need some additional time when you mail to them. Add about two or three weeks.

Registering People

When people show up to attend the seminar/workshop that you give, there must be a system to get them "registered." This means you need to check them off a list of those who are pre-registered or take their payment as a walk-in if they are not yet registered.

With the people who are pre-registered and pre-paid, the only thing you will have to do is check them off the list and give them a receipt. If they haven't made payment, you need to have a system to take payment and give them some sort of receipt.

After they are registered, you also need to give people whatever handouts or materials they will be getting for the event.

If you are doing a small group of 25 or less, you can handle registration yourself with a minimum of problems. Have a good list of all of those registered to that point. Also make sure that next to the name you indicated whether or not they have paid and by what means.

If they paid by credit card, give them their credit card receipts. What we do is to have a small envelope inside each folder for each seminar. After we process the credit cards, we open the file folder and put the receipts inside a smaller envelope that we put inside the folder.

I like the idea of having a registration table out in front of the room where you are holding the event. Make sure that you have names and name tags laid out in alphabetical order on the table. This way people can quickly and easily find their name and/or materials for the seminar.

You don't need to look high tech, but you do need to look organized. If you don't, it will hurt you both in terms of perception and in not getting all you fully deserve.

You will also have a certain number of people at a large seminar that will try to sneak in for free. Be aware of this fact and set up your systems to prevent this from happening.

800 Numbers to Register

Using an 800 number will increase registration numbers, particularly when those calling are from outside your own area. It also makes you look bigger than maybe you are. In most cases, this will be helpful.

The research in this area is conclusive. Providing an 800 number will significantly increase registration numbers. If you don't have one, get one.

Answering the Phones

If you have more than one business, or type of business operating out of one office, you may need to use a rather generic greeting, particularly if you are dealing with more than one niche market.

I answer the phone, "Hello, Fred speaking. How can I help you?"

The next questions asked are done to try to figure out which market niche they are calling about. I don't want to start selling someone on my brilliance in helping video producers if I am speaking to a caterer. It has happened.

One way to do this is to assign extension numbers to any ads you place with a standard toll free number that rings in your office. So when people ask for extension 101, you or your assistant can say, "Yes, can I help you". But you will know what market they are calling from at that point and know how to proceed.

If people are inquiring about a seminar we never immediately say that a seat is available. We ask them which city they are calling about if we are promoting multiple dates. Then we ask them to hold on while we check if we still have space available. This creates the feeling that a lot of people have been calling and there is heavy demand.

You must create this feeling. If not, people will not want to come. No one wants to go to an event where very few people will attend. For some reason they feel it won't be that good.

The key here is to give people the feeling of scarcity. By making something seem like it is in heavy demand, it gets people to make a decision more quickly. It also makes them less likely to quibble about price.

If a meeting planner or a client is calling, I never try to act inaccessible. If I am in the office, I will always take their calls.

Live Operator/Voice Mail

When people call to register, they are much more likely to sign up if they speak to a live person. For registration, I highly recommend that you have a live person answering the phones. If they reach you after hours or when no one is around to answer, have a good machine to take the messages and return these calls promptly. If you don't, you'll lose money.

The "Heart Attack" Seminar Registration Curve

People who have never done seminars before experience an incredible amount of anxiety and stress. They stress over the fact that registrations come in at a very odd pace. They generally come in slowly at first and then dramatically pick up within a week or so of the seminar date. I call it the heart attack curve because the uninformed person freaks out waiting for the registrations. Sometimes you get as much as 50% or more of your registrations in the last five to seven days before the date of the seminar.

A variety of factors will affect your registration curve. Your goal for both your health and your cash flow will be to smooth out this curve as much as possible.

In general, the more expensive your seminar, the earlier people will register. Seldom do people wait until the last minute to make a big dollar decision regarding a seminar. You should also be promoting it further in advance.

The longer your seminar, the earlier your registrations will generally come in. If you have a three day seminar, your promotional material will go out earlier. This, in addition to people having to plan further in advance, will usually make registrations come in sooner.

You can sometimes smooth out the enrollment curve by offering incentives for early enrollment. The one I always use is to offer people 10% off if they register more than 3 weeks before the seminar will take place.

Others offer a step stair discount based on the dates people register. People might be asked to pay $350 by May 1st, $400 by May 15th and $450 by May 30th. Think about testing a similar system to see what works for you.

Getting Paid at Your Seminars

Taking Credit Cards

Taking credit cards for payment of the seminar registration fee will help to increase the number of people who sign up. If you don't take credit cards, you need to get set up to do so or you will lose money.

Call Card Service International at 1-800-675-6573 to get set up. If you tell them that I sent you and mention this book they will give you a substantial discount. They specialized in working with speakers and other entrepreneurs who usually have a hard time getting accepted to receive a merchant account.

Accepting Checks

Some speakers and seminar promoters will tell you not to accept checks. I say baloney. Will you occasionally get stiffed? Absolutely. It's the cost of doing business.

Try to make it as easy as possible for people to do business with you. That includes allowing people to pay you by check. In all the years I have been doing business I can count on two hands all the bad checks I have received. Of the less than ten that I have gotten, all but two of the individuals made good on the money they owed me. Take checks! It makes sense!

Cash

Never refuse cash at anytime, anywhere! Be sure to report it on your taxes.

Name Tags

Some people think name tags are sort of hokey. I like using them. I am usually pretty good at names, but I sometimes need some help.

Use them at your events and ask people to put their first names in big letters and last name underneath it.

Also, make sure they don't ruin peoples' clothes.

Interacting with Hotels for Seminars

Many of your events (either speeches or seminars) will be held at hotels. This being the case, I wanted to give you some suggestions that might help you in dealing with these folks.

Unless you are doing a seminar where you expect to have a lot of people, you will probably be dealing with the catering department. The sales department only comes into play if you are booking sleeping rooms. Usually when you book a lot of sleeping rooms, the hotel will give you the meeting rooms for free.

If you aren't using a lot of sleeping rooms, call sales and let them direct you to the right party.

I also like to deal directly with a given hotel property as opposed to going through the national toll free number. They may claim that they can book a meeting space, but it usually ends up being a logistical nightmare. Go direct and you'll be much happier.

Always request less space than you need. This will get you the best price. If you say you need space for 35 people they will give you the same room (in most cases) that they would have given you if you asked for a room for 45 people. If 45 people show up, then you will just have to squeeze in some chairs. They won't charge you any more for the space.

If you do need to move to a larger room, try to continue to plead poverty for your best rates.

Always check your room the night before your event. You will usually find something has to be moved or changed.

Never use any audio-video equipment from the hotel. It is a complete rip off. If you must get a hold of this type of equipment, contract for it on your own or bring it with you, if at all possible.

If you need simple stuff, I have had good luck with the national rental places like Rent-a-Center. Call them for your basic TVs and VCRs.

Eating on site is a lot easier than going out to eat. It is often more expensive to eat at the hotel, but the problem is that you are frequently on a tight time schedule. This makes getting in a car and going to a restaurant a minimum 90 minute ordeal. You can usually eat at the hotel in 45 minutes or less.

If there is a restaurant in the hotel, you may want to take the whole group over and save yourself a few bucks. It will normally be less than having them bring the food to the meeting room. I also like getting out of the meeting room for the meal.

Never pay your bill without carefully checking it out. For some reason the mistakes, when they are made (which is often,) never seem to be made in your favor. I would estimate that they attempt to overcharge me at least 35% of the time I use a hotel to do seminars.

Should you provide refreshments? I always like to have coffee and a few donuts in the morning. I also like to have a collection of sodas after lunch. The more expensive your seminar, the better the treats you should put out at the breaks.

Setting Up the Rooms Where You Speak

If you are in control of how your room where you will be speaking is set up, there are some things you need to know.

Theatre Style

This is where people are sitting on chairs, generally with no armrests and too close together. This se- up is best when you are doing a short program of less than two hours. Sitting in chairs like this for more than that length of time gets people really annoyed.

Trust me, when I worked with CareerTrack, they used to have the rooms set this way all the time. One of the reasons is that it costs less because you can get more people into the same size room and the amount of time required to set up is less. If you have any control over set-up, don't let them set it up this way for any presentation over 90 minutes or so. Also, leave at least 6 – 9 inches between the chairs.

Classroom Style

This is where every seat has a table for writing on it. This is great for any speech, or more likely a seminar where people will have to do a significant amount of note taking.

You will not be able to accommodate as many people using this set-up as you would using theatre style seating, but for anything over 90 minutes, where any note taking is required, it is a must.

Group exercises are a little tougher to do, but can still be done fairly easily. Ask the hotel or meeting space that you use to leave some room in between the table,s if at all possible.

Round Tables

Round tables are a great way to set up a room. I like it because it is informal and easy for doing group exercises. If you are going to be doing a lot of group work in your presentation, and space isn't a problem, use round tables.

U-Shaped

Setting up in a U-Shape is great for very small groups of 25 or less. It is a good choice when there will be a lot of writing and audience participation is encouraged.

Always be in the Room Early

Something will always go wrong with logistics at a seminar or a speech. Expect it. The best way to deal with these types of problems is to get to the room early. This way you'll be able to correct any issues which arise well in advance.

I try to show up at the room or location at least 45 minutes in advance., not only to check on all the various logistics, but also to get a feel for the room. This will make it much easier for me to feel comfortable doing my presentation before I even start.

On the logistics side, here are some things that you must check.

■ Is the mike working that they have assigned to you?

■ Do you have a back up available?

■ Do the various other pieces of equipment necessary for your presentation work? (Overhead projector, screen projecting device, etc.)

■ Do you have water and lemon close to your speaking area?

■ Are your handouts easily accessible?

■ Do you have back up copies of your handouts in case more people show up?

There will always be some problems. Expect them. Don't let them rattle you. Just have a plan to deal with all the various options.

Handouts/Workbooks

The proper design of your handouts and workbooks are essential to success in the seminar business. These are the items you give to people when they come to attend your seminars.

I have seen another marketing "guru" give a high priced seminar and not use a single handout. No handouts, no nothing! This makes no sense to me. I had to conclude one of two things about his tactic. Either he was lazy or he had some secret motive for doing things this way. To this day I have not been able to see any way that it was done as a tactical move. Draw your own conclusions.

The outline that you created for the seminar becomes the skeleton for your workbook. Make it an outline and include some of the subpoints under each major topic. The best handouts are at least mildly interactive. The best way to do this is to use a fill in the blank system. Not every single line needs to be done this way, but make it a mixture of straight information and places where participants need to do a little bit of work. You may also want to include some mini tests or quizzes for them to take.

Include relevant samples and examples at the end of the workbook. Any articles and other supporting material should also be placed at the back.

Something I have learned the hard way is that the workbook pages must be numbered. I like the idea of using letters to identify all the samples in the appendix. Having tried to get people to look for things in the manual without a numbering scheme, I don't recommend it. You'll hear about it on the evaluations if you don't number.

Never attach your order sheet to the handout you give to people at the beginning of a class. I just attended a workshop in which this was done. It will not help you to maximize your numbers in the sales of your various products.

No matter how short your presentation, you need to have a handout. This must be done for two primary reasons: first, to prove to your audience and the folks who booked you that you delivered usable content and information.

The second is a marketing reason. You need to give people a way to get in touch with you after the event. Naturally, your contact information must be somewhere on the handout. I also like to include a very extensive bibliography. I include every single book that I know or have heard of that has a reference to the subject.

Whenever I do a full day or multi-day seminar, I like to put a few things up in the front of the manual for starters. I always include a bio about myself and a list of objectives for the session.

The bio you include should make people absolutely convinced that you are the right person to be doing the work. Your list of objectives should closely match what you advertised to get people to attend. If not, you're going to have problems.

Some people like to color code their handouts. This seems like a great idea, but I have never been quite that ambitious. If you have the time to do this, I suspect you should be spending more time on seminar content and information.

At the end of any seminar manual, you need to give a full list of resources. These resources should be both your own and those that others can provide.

When you list what you can provide your participants, don't be shy. Tell people what you can do for them and in what areas. Tell attendees how you can help them with your products by giving them a list and describing how each product will help them if they buy them. Give them specifics.

Describe how your consulting services work and how people can take advantage of them if they decide to.

Remember that your handout should not just be geared to giving people great information, but to maximizing your profitability.

Evaluations

If at all possible, try to give out evaluations at the end of every speech or seminar, not just to get the customary feedback you may be thinking of, but for a number of other very important reasons.

First, you need to be able to quantify your results. Second, an evaluation is your best opportunity to get great quotes you can use in your promotional material. I remind people about the section in my evaluations which asks them to list what they liked best and least about the session. I tell them that, if they liked my presentation and want to put down something positive, to please be specific. This will help me get the quotes that are the most powerful and best to use. Third, it is also a great place to get referral business.

There should also be a section in which you ask people if they would be interested in certain kinds of additional services. Any of these items that are ticked off should be followed up quickly. They indicate a very clear opportunity for additional revenue from a source that is very favorably pre-disposed in your direction.

To get the maximum amount of returns on your evaluations, do two things. First, try to give participants some small incentive for filling them out. Also, make sure and get them into peoples' hands before the end of your presentation.

If you only have an hour, try to give them some time right before you finish, if at all possible.

Any evaluation you use should have a section where they can sign it and let you use their comments in your promotional material. This is very important. The more positive comments you can get, the better. Ask for a signature that gives you that "release." That way you will have yourself protected. Don't lose these originals. Put them in a very safe place.

There should also be a place where you ask people whether or not they are interested in other items that you offer. This will make it much easier for you to follow up and make money from your related products and services.

Keep the evaluation very simple using a 1 to 10 scale. Everyone knows how to use this scale and it is the easiest to tabulate. Let people know if one is high or low. My suggestion is to make one the low, or the worst, and 10 the high, or the best. To do otherwise is counterintuitive and your results will be a little wacky.

Also, make it easy for people to fill out your evaluations. I used to have people circle the number. Now I have a new fancy scanner where I ask people to fill in the dots. If you have a lot of evaluations, this will severely reduce your workload.

Leave room for comments. That way people will have plenty of room to sing your praises. The quotes that I get on my evaluations are absolutely essential to my promotional efforts. You need them as well.

In the event that you get some negative responses on these evaluations, don't let it bother you. There are a certain number of people out there who are just impossible to please. Don't even try to make them happy. They are unhappy people to begin with. Don't let them bother you after the fact with their evaluations.

Occasionally someone will really SLAM you in an evaluation. Unless you see it happen frequently, laugh at these.

Unless you get a lot of negative evaluations (over 5%), don't worry about it. Do read the negative ones if you have the stomach. Every once in a while they have a grain of truth worth responding to. But always remember, you can't please all of the people, all of the time.

Also ask people to give you a list of other topics they would like to have you speak to them about. This will set you up for trying to get repeat business from this client.

I've included a sample of my evaluation for you to view.

Your Goal at a Seminar

I have three goals when I give a seminar. First, I want to get great evaluations. Second, I want to sell a lot of product. Third, I want to achieve both of these goals in such a way that people will enthusiastically want to do business with me again and again.

All three items are very measurable. This is crucial. I don't want any of my goals to be subjective and murky. How can you tell whether or not you are achieving goals that aren't well defined? You can't. Plain and simple.

I suggest you ask yourself the same questions with regards to the seminars that you do. How will you determine if your seminars are successful? Have all the items be measurable.

Evaluations will tell you whether or not people like and respect you. Numbers on product sales will tell you whether or not this is the case.

Starting the Seminar

The first thing you should always do is to start on time. Do not penalize those who got to the meeting location on time by starting late.

I make this very clear in all of my promotional literature that we start and end exactly on time. I also put this on the confirmation I send to people. People will respect you for doing this, even those who come late.

You may not be able to be this rigid when you are speaking for an organization at one of their events. But let your host know how important you feel it is to start on time.

At the start of the session, I like to have everyone go around the room and briefly introduce themselves. I do my own introduction last. I ask people to be brief (30 seconds or so) and I cut them off gently if they get long-winded.

This gives everyone in the group a chance to hear who is in attendance. Since I am very insistent on starting exactly on time, this lets the late comers arrive without interrupting any formal procedure.

While people are introducing themselves, take notes. This will allow you to take down any relevant information for future use.

It is also perfectly appropriate to make some quick and pithy comments on what your participants say in their introductions. Just don't use up all of the time to highlight your own comedic brilliance.

I listen carefully as people go around the room. I take notes onto the roster. I suggest you do the same. This will be invaluable to you in the future.

After you go around the room, you need to introduce yourself. This is an important step to establish credibility. To do this you don't have to go so far back as to let people know who your third grade teacher was. But do include any and everything you can to show that you are the expert in the topic you are dealing with on that day.

Your self-introductions depend on your topic. Different topics, different introductions.

The first few minutes you spend in front of a group are crucial. This is where you establish the relationship that people will not forget. Your goal is to get people to both like and respect you. It is also to set the stage for making sure that you sell a boat load of product.

Modular Content System

After you master the marketing side of the speaking business, you need to have something of value to say when you are asked to speak.

The modular content system is a method I developed that will allow you to develop speech and seminar content that is easily insertable into any speech or seminar you give.

The best way to imagine the modules are like individual records on a large jukebox. You can then pick which records to play at any presentation and what order you will play them in.

Each module I create starts with a major point. Let's say I am creating a module for customer service. My major point is to "fully engage" any customer you come into contact with.

When I first started doing this, I put each module on an index card. Now they go into the computer. I will start with that major point and then think of any subpoints I would like to discuss to support the main point. I try to limit the number of subpoints to no more than four or five.

I will then write down any and all stories I can think of that can prove or support this point. These are stories about myself or stories about others. If I have a prop that I can use to illustrate this point, I note it under the major point.

Are there any quotes that I currently have that I can use to support this major point? If not, I will leave a blank and then put a quote in when I find one by chance at some future date.

If there is a magic trick that might be appropriate to support this major point, that will also go in this area.

I have over 350 modules on various topics that I can use in any speech or seminar. Picture this as a jukebox of information that I can now assemble into an album (for those of you who remember what those are) of music that I can then "play" for my audience.

I have each of these modules available to me to use at a moment's notice. Of course I am always developing new modules whenever they come to me.

I suggest that you start to think modularly. Think using this system or developing a system like this to catalogue your knowledge and information in a way that will be easy for you to access and add to.

Get started immediately putting together your system; your life will be much easier as a speaker.

Audience Involvement

With any presentation you give, even a keynote speech, you want to get your audience involved. The reason for this is something I call the "sing-a-long" syndrome in the speaking business. When musical performers use a lot of sing-a-longs in their music act, these events are rated much higher in terms of audience evaluation.

Do I have any research to back this up? ABSOLUTELY NOT! It is just a gut feeling, but I'm confident that I am right. Why? Because I have looked at my own evaluations when I have used and not used audience participation of some kind during a presentation or seminar.

Ratings are almost always higher when the audience has gotten involved. If you want to see the same in a music act, just go to a Jimmy Buffet concert and ask the fans how they liked the concert after the show. He is consistently rated as one of the best liked performers and I think it is 90% related to the fact that people are singing along with 90% of the songs he plays.

In a shorter presentation, you will have much less time to use this technique. But you still need to use it, even at a very minimal level.

A good rule of thumb is to have audience involvement, in some manner, shape, or form, at least once every two hours in a seminar. Try to limit these exercises to a maximum of 10 minutes at a time. This is the absolute maximum length. Going any longer gets completely unruly and totally out of hand.

When you have a seminar of at least three or four hours, I like to break people up into groups. Keep your group between four and six. The easiest way to do this is to set the room up with round tables that hold no more than six. Then your groups are automatically set up.

If you have time, you may want to hand out numbers that go from one to five. Then ask everyone to arrange themselves into groups with one of each number in their group. Always give people a time frame of no more than 45 seconds to get themselves into a group.

After you get people into groups, you then need to select a group leader. I tell people to select the person whose birthday is closest to January 1st. Or I tell them that the person with the newest looking shoes is their group's leader. Selecting a leader will make it fun.

When you want to get an answer from an audience, ask people to stand up and sit down in answer to questions that you ask. This gives you both the answer to questions you are asking, and also allows for you to break up your groups.

Audience involvement is crucial to making your speeches and seminars work. Incorporate it into any presentation you do.

People Believe Their Own Data

When you do seminars, there is always a tendency on your part to give people the information that you have, rather than letting them discover it themselves.

Use exercises to let people discover what you want them to know. It may not make you look quite as impressive, but it does have a much stronger impact on your audience members.

Stay on Schedule

As a participant in many a seminar myself, there is nothing I hate worse than having a person ask a question that is way off the topic and the speaker taking the time to answer it. Many times this pulls the seminar way off the schedule and makes it impossible to cover information that was promised in the promotional material.

As a seminar leader and speaker, you need to know what should and shouldn't be answered. You need to be sure you never stray too far off course and thus leave out material that people expect you to cover.

Also, keep yourself on a tight time schedule. If you don't, people will be annoyed, angry and won't buy as much product from you or give you evaluations that are as high. Try not to veer more than five minutes off schedule at any time.

Always Repeat Questions Asked

One of the most annoying things for a member of any audience is to only hear the answer to a question asked by another audience member. As the speaker, you must learn to repeat questions asked by your audience before answering them. If you do this, people won't notice. If you don't, they will. And they will be annoyed.

It is also great training for when you start creating products. To not repeat questions when asked about producing a product is not just unforgivable, it is deadly. That issue alone will cause your return rates on products to increase.

From now on make it a rule to repeat every question you get asked.

Introductions

When you are going to speak, it is important that you know exactly how your introduction will go. The reason is that this is really the beginning of your speech. It will set the tone for the rest of your prepared remarks. For this reason, you can't afford any surprises. I have often been at events where a glib (occasionally intoxicated) member of the company was given the job of introducing the speaker.

In order for you to not have any surprises, you need to have a standard introduction prepared. This way you will know exactly what is coming and what to say when you take the stage.

This introduction should be double spaced in fairly large print and preferably put on one sheet of paper. This way your introducer will have no problem reading it. Make sure that you put it in a font that is easy to read like Times Roman or Garamond. Do not use a Sans Serif type like Helvetica or Arial.

Never Give Exact Times for Topics

If you list the topics to be covered at your seminar, never put exact times as to when the items will be covered. What you can do is put the items in the order they will be covered and divide them into a morning and afternoon line up. The reason why you should not put times next to each of your items is this: Someone will look at his or her watch and say, "It's 10:30; why aren't we covering this?" This is deadly. Don't lock yourself into a time frame.

Things happen during the course of the seminar which may cause you to go longer or shorter when covering certain topics. Even if you have done the seminar 50 times before, this may still happen. A given group may need more or less concentration on a given issue. Keep yourself flexible.

Index Card Concept

A great idea I picked up at a seminar goes like this. When you first start the seminar, ask everyone to write down on an index card (which you provide) the most important question that they would like to get answered at the seminar.

At any time during the seminar, when someone gets their main question answered, they are asked to stand, tear up their index cards and announce to the rest of the group what their question was and how it was just answered.

This does a couple of great things for your seminar. First, it breaks up the day by having someone do something physical. By standing, you break up the day right there. By giving the question and how it was answered, you further reinforce that particular point of content.

If a participant had that particular question down as their MOST IMPORTANT question, it certainly bares reinforcing. Doing it in the way that I just described makes a lot of sense.

Use a "Content Action Idea Sheet"

At the beginning of every seminar I always create something that I call the "content action idea" sheet. It is a one page sheet that has bullet points all down the left hand side of the page. For a full day seminar there are about 20 bullet points.

People who come to a seminar or workshop expect a minimum of two things: a good speaker and good content. One without the other is not enough. If you have good presentation skills, then you need to concentrate on delivering content value.

Ask your audience members to write down the ideas they find worth taking home with them on the action idea sheet. I actually promise people that they will have three great ideas by the lunch break or they should come to me and ask for their money back.

If you can't back it up, don't make this kind of statement.

I then review the contact action idea sheet a few times during the day, usually after each break. This further reinforces the best elements of the seminar.

At the end of the day I ask people to look at all of their content action ideas and put an "A", "B" or "C" next to each of the content points. I have them do this based on ideas they can start to implement within the next week, the next month and the next three months.

As the final exercise of the seminar I go around the room (if it is a group of less than 50) and ask them to shout out the best idea they got out of the seminar. I tell them that if someone else uses the one that they were going to use that they must select another one. This way, I show people how much content I delivered as the final exercise. It's an impressive exercise to show people how much content you truly delivered.

Make it Fun

Most people expect a seminar to be boring. Surprise them. Make it fun, yet pack it with immediately useable content. This will surprise anyone who attends.

Breaks

In a seminar of any length I like to give breaks every hour or so. I always tell people that it is a short break. Never go more than 90 minutes. There is a reason why college classes run 50 minutes.

If you have to cram a mass of information into a short period of time, just make sure to give people short breaks to keep their attention. People who ignore this rule will get hurt in the evaluations and in product sales as well. Remember your over-riding goals. Take breaks and keep people comfortable. It will keep people buying as well.

Adults Learn Best Using Kid Techniques

One of the best ways to keep people interested during a speech or seminar is to remember that adults learn best when you use the same techniques that are effective when working with children.

If you don't remember it yourself, go to all of the kindergarten teachers you know and ask them what teaching techniques work with their kids. Most of these will be effective with adults.

Not long ago at a small group, one day seminar with a Fortune 500 company I had a dozen high powered corporate executives down on the floor working with Legos.

The Post-it Note System for Questions

There will be times during your seminar when you will not want to answer a question at that particular time. People will be frustrated if they can't put their question down, even if it will be answered later.

Here's the best way to handle this. Put post-it notes on every table at your seminar. When people have a question that you don't want to answer at that particular point in time, ask them to write the question on a post-it and then put it up on the board that you call the "Later" board or some other clever name.

This accomplishes your two key objectives as a speaker with regards to postponed questions. First, people are allowed to get their questions out of their heads and onto paper and second, you as a speaker can determine when you want to answer the questions by visiting the board at each break and pulling all of the post-its down. Bring them up to the front of the room with you and answer them when appropriate.

All Exercises Must Prove a Point

Never do any kind of an exercise where people are left wondering why you did something and what it proved. Every exercise must prove a point. Don't do this and risk looking foolish.

Many speakers will do some kind of an "icebreaker" to loosen people up at the beginning of a seminar. Virtually any exercise will get people loosened up, so choose one that proves a point.

Guest Speakers

Getting guest speakers on board at your events will increase the perception of value of the seminar that you offer. In addition to providing additional values through guest speakers, you should also generate some more cash. Speakers you ask to speak will most likely have product that they sell.

The financial arrangements usually work by giving the speaker a guarantee against product sales that you split. Let's say the person has a product that they sell for $500. You get 50% of the revenue they generate. But you have to guarantee them at least $3,000 for the appearance. This works if you have enough people to make sure you can generate more revenue than the guarantee amount. That way, each of the guest speakers is paying their own way as an absolute minimum.

Do not work this arrangement without having seen the person in action in front of another group. Never make a guarantee of any amount of money without doing your due diligence to find out whether you are dealing with someone with great content and exceptional product sales ability.

Want to use me at your event? I love this kind of arrangement. Call me.

Hot Seats

This is a concept that I have seen used in many seminars or workshops that I feel is very effective. You set aside time, usually towards the end of the session to bring a certain number of people up in front of the entire group.

You ask them to briefly introduce themselves. Then you ask them to share their biggest problem with the group. Then you give your best suggestions to the person up in front of the group. Then allow other participants, for a short time, to offer their suggestions. Jump in if they get too far off track from what makes sense. If you are doing the seminar, workshop or bootcamp with someone else, do the first part of this exercise jointly. This works out extremely well because it allows for you to answer specific questions from individual members. It increases the value of your meeting by a measurable degree. It is as close as you can get to giving people individual assistance.

Many bootcamps and seminars will encourage early enrollment for an event by offering only a limited number of hot seats. They are given out on a first come, first served basis. This has been very effective in getting me to sign up for a number of events.

Speaking of individual assistance, I have attended a seminar which sold me on attending with the following promise: that I would receive, in addition to everything else, a one on one consultation with the seminar guru. This is a great way to add additional appeal to the event and justify the high price you are charging. You will also want to go longer than an eight hour day. This will make people feel like they got greater value for the dollar.

I also like the idea of planning at least one "big event" for the group. In my case, with an office in New York City it is usually a Broadway show. I make it optional and people have to pay for it themselves. There is usually no resistance to the fact that they have to pay since they are already paying quite a bit to be there. Some people go, others choose to do other things.

If you have a lot of people, it may be impossible for you to offer the hot seat experience to everyone. In order to do this equitably you can allow those who register first to get the first crack at a hot seat. Doing it this way builds the value of the hot seat and allows you an easy selection process based on when people register.

Bootcamps

The term bootcamp is used to describe a high priced, multi-day seminar that concentrates on nuts and bolts "how to" information.

These are best promoted to an in-house list of people who have purchased from you before. It is difficult to get people to drop a lot of cash for a two to three day seminar unless they have seen you in action before.

The exception to this rule is if you have already established yourself as a celebrity within this niche. In that case, it may make sense for you to promote bootcamp to everyone in the industry.

Bootcamps are usually priced at a minimum of $500 a day. A three day bootcamp would then have a minimum price point of around $1500. Many are priced at many times that.

You intentionally want to make this an elitist event based on the pricing. Make it fairly inexpensive for people to bring additional people, spouses or other employees, to sit in on the presentation.

Earlier this summer I went to a bootcamp myself on commodity trading that was priced at $4995. Lots of money? Sure! Worth it? Absolutely! The only way to find out what price to charge for your bootcamps is by testing. And when you do price testing, it is always a good idea to start at a higher number than you think people will pay. You can always start discounting after that.

Your primary means of promoting your bootcamp will be through a long form sales letter that details all the many benefits that people will get from attending.

Once you get people to the bootcamp there is a good chance that there will be a high percentage of potential consulting clients in the group. They've paid a lot of money to be there, so they are pre-qualified. This is another great financial benefit of holding bootcamps.

You will want to try to get a number of guest speakers and you'll definitely want to use hot seats. The outside speakers should be people you find who have specific areas of expertise that would be of interest to your attendees, expertise that you either don't have yourself or that you want someone to embellish on. Make sure that you have at least one guest speaker per day. This will help decrease the boredom factor that people might have if they were just listening to you.

Do you compensate the speakers? No, not directly. Find people who are willing to come speak to your group because they have something to sell to your group. What they have to sell may be products or services. You will want to get a piece of whatever they sell to your group. A 50-50 split is not unusual on any products sold at the event.

Make sure you have heard them speak and have seen them pitch their services. I recently invited someone to speak at one of my events. I would never use him again. Why? He was a weak speaker and his information wasn't tailored to meet our group's concern. He hadn't done his homework on the storage industry. The result: I looked bad.

Naturally, when you do the bootcamp, make sure you record it. You can sell the tapes and make a bundle. I have sold many a set of bootcamp tapes at a minimum of $497. In addition, since you are promoting this to a small group of existing customers, your cost of promotion is extremely low.

One of the nicest things about bootcamps is that you usually don't have to travel. Hold the event in your home city. People come to you and they'll pay a lot of money to be there. This assumes that you're in a location that's reasonably easy to get to and somewhat appealing. I am not saying that if you live in Bismarck, North Dakota, it will be impossible for you to get people to come to you, but you would be better advised to have everyone go to Aspen, instead.

I hold bootcamps for speakers on a regular basis in both New York City and the Las Vegas area. I do these at times of the year where these cities are most attractive to visitors. The Las Vegas event is held in the winter and the New York City event is held in either June or October or both.

If you've taken good care of your customers, you can count on between 5% – 10% of the people to sign up for your high-priced bootcamp.

Let's say you had 500 customers. This means that if you sent a bootcamp solicitation to your database you could expect to get somewhere between 25 and 50 people to attend. They will give you $1,495 for a three days session where they come to sit at the feet of you, the guru of whatever it is that you do.

How do you promote a bootcamp? With a series of long sales letters starting about 10 to 12 weeks before the event. It is both a high priced event and it requires that most people travel to get there. Therefore, you must give people plenty of time to think about it and book travel plans and get good airfares.

I suggest you start by sending people a long and detailed sales letter. Then follow up with another fairly long sales letter two weeks later. Follow up with another 4 page letter two weeks after that. Then send a final postcard one week after that. This will get as many people as you can get to come.

The first thing you need to do is to find a local hotel. Get a room that will hold the appropriate amount of people based on the computations you make from the information I've given you above.

Sponsored Seminars

Another way you can get paid to do seminars is by finding a corporate sponsor. If you can get an organization to sponsor your seminar, this is certainly worth considering.

Let's say that you are a speaker on corporate diversity. If you are approached by a company like Denny's (who has had a problem that they have forcefully addressed in this area), it is worth sitting down with them to have a serious discussion.

I haven't had one of my seminars sponsored myself, but I have talked to numerous speakers who have. There seem to be a lot of different arrangements that I have heard about. If you are approached, I am sure it won't be exactly what I describe to you here, but it may be somewhat close.

You may be offered a flat daily rate, plus your travel expenses, but you will be responsible for the marketing of the seminar. You may be asked to just show up and the company will pick up your travel tab and give you a flat daily rate. They may also offer you a flat daily rate and split the product sales with you.

The best way to see if you are getting offered a good deal is to compute what you normally make per engagement at any speech or seminar that you do (including product sales) and compare it to what they are willing to offer.

If they ask you what you think is reasonable, start with that same number and see if you can get an additional 20% or so.

You need to take a look at any arrangement a sponsor offers you. I would never let sponsored seminars take up your entire schedule, but it will certainly help you pay a lot of bills.

Room Set-up Sheet

You will need to send a sheet to your client letting them know exactly how you want your room set up.

Don't be surprised or annoyed if it isn't set up that way when you arrive. This happens all the time. The way you respond will be duly noted by your host or hostess.

Also, if you really want to make points with your host, offer to help change the set up if done incorrectly. They will almost always refuse your offer, but they'll be impressed that you didn't feel like you were too much of a big shot to ask.

Give as much detail as you can for your room set up. Include a graphic which gives a pictorial representation of where you want things positioned. A picture will always help to get things right.

Treat the staff at the hotel with the utmost courtesy and respect. To be very honest, many speakers are extremely arrogant and demanding of hotel staff. This gives US a bad name in general with this group. Treat them well and they will respond in kind! I even tip the staff with my own money. A buck or two is no skin off your back and they will run circles for you during the time you are there.

Let them know if you want a remote or corded mike. Do you prefer a lavaliere or hand held mike?

Make sure and ask for back-up batteries. I even like to bring a few of my own, just in case.

If at all possible, check the room you will be speaking in as soon as you arrive. If you come in the evening before, ask to speak to a manager on duty. Let them know you are the first speaker in the morning and want to get access to the room. They will usually be very accommodating.

Keep a cell phone number for your contact handy, just in case!

Always show up for your event at least 30 – 60 minutes ahead of your speaking time. This is for two reasons. First, you want to make sure everything is working right. Second, you want to listen to the speaker right before you. This will allow you to play off any of what they said in your speech.

Many speakers show up two minutes beforehand. They are not even aware of what was said before they went on; this is dumb. If the previous speaker made a reference and you aren't there, it could be embarrassing. Be careful. Be there!

Video/Audio Taping Your Seminar

There are two areas to talk about here: your policy regarding others taping your events and how you record your own seminars.

Don't ever allow people to audio tape the seminars you do. You need to have this policy in writing on your contract and handout materials. You also need to mention it quickly at the beginning of the seminar when you do your housekeeping schpiel. You don't want people to tape you for two reasons.

First, you want to sell products to them. Second, the quality of your recorded word will be suspect. Let's assume that someone shows up at your seminar with a walkman. They tape your seminar. The tape gets distributed The quality of the sound will be lousy. This will make you look bad. Not good.

Recording Your Own Seminars

Please don't make the same mistake I did on this one. I have produced many audio and video cassette training programs. For many years I produced exclusively audio programs. I never spent the time and bought a good audio recording device. This was a huge mistake.

Bite the bullet and buy a professional recording device and a good mike. I use a Marantz deck. I also bought a $100 mike. The total was about $450. The net result, if you do things this way, will be the following. You will be able to get a good clean "master" of your presentation.

You will then be able to duplicate it "as is" or edit the final product. Trust me on this one. Spend the money now. You will make your money back when you sell your first set of products. This is well worth it. Do it!

Let's talk about video. Occasionally you will be asked by a corporate client if they can tape your presentation. I always say yes to this as long as they will give me a good copy of the masters.

There are some really horrible videos that are floating around out there. I have been to numerous seminars given by supposed gurus in the field of information product marketing who will say something different. I believe you must have a decent looking product to sell to people.

This doesn't mean you have to spend the money to produce a Hollywood style video. It should be somewhere between that point and looking like you did the video on your personal camcorder.

I don't want you to spend big money on video productions. I want you to spend enough money to make those people who buy impressed enough that they will buy more. They must be most impressed with the content of the video. But we don't want them to be distracted by how bad the presentation is.

Take Notes While Giving the Seminar

Participants will improve your seminar each time you give it. The key is that you keep your instructors manual next to you. When someone brings up a point that you either haven't thought of or haven't included, you need to take notes in the appropriate area in your manual. You will make those changes the next time you do the seminar. That way, each time you do the seminar, it will improve.

By the time you have given the seminar 30 times, you will have it down fairly tightly with all the great additional ideas coming from your seminar attendees. However, to this day, I still walk into a room with a group every once in a while and get a great idea from a seminar participant.

When there are significant changes, you may want to change your workbooks or handouts to reflect the changes your audience has told you to make.

Don't do what I have done in the past. That is to <u>think</u> to yourself that you will have to change or include certain things the next time you do the seminar. You won't. You'll forget. The net result will be a lot of frustration on your part and a less improved seminar.

So keep your pen handy at all times! Write it down whenever you get a great idea. That will forget anything slipping through the cracks.

Certificates of Completion

Your seminar participants will be tremendously impressed if you give them a very simple but inexpensive certificate of completion.

I don't know why, but some people get all excited about this kind of acknowledgment. This is usually the case with lower level employees. But remember, it doesn't matter what you think or feel; it's what your participants think or feel that counts.

If they like it, give it to them. The cost is so minimal and creates such goodwill.

There are a number of software programs out there that will allow you to create very attractive certificates that you can then print on a variety of different kinds of paper, depending on how fancy you want to make them.

I recommend you use these for any program that is a day or longer in length. They don't cost much and clients love them.

Dealing with a Dissatisfied Participant

If someone isn't happy at your seminar, try to pull them aside from the rest of your group at the break. See if you can make them happy regardless of what you do. If you can, and think this will satisfy them, then do it. If you feel you can't make them happy, invite them to leave. Give them their money back and send them on their way.

Do not let a problem person infect the rest of the group. Get them out of there!

Pre-Program Questionnaire

In order to give the best speech to any group, you need to get as much pertinent information as possible before the fact. This will give you information you need to customize your speech and make it that much more memorable and effective.

You should do this not just to make the individual group you are speaking to happy about that particular speech, but so they will ask you back again and refer you to others.

Part of that pre-program questionnaire should include a request for names of people you can interview who represent various factions of the group you will be speaking to. Many speakers pay lip service to customization of their speeches, but few actually do it.

To be honest, those speakers who do this right don't spend an inordinate amount of time customizing. Nor should you. It would be a waste of your time to OVER customize. But it is very much in your best interest to do an adequate amount of customization.

That would mean calling at least four or five people from different representative factions within the group to which you will be speaking. Your contact at the corporation or association will try to give you the "best" people from each of these groups. Try to get him or her to give you a person who they feel is a true representative from each faction of the group.

This will be tough to get. They usually want to give you their best, rather than their average people.

Be aware of one very important thing; if you ask for names of people to call and then don't call them, you will look like a fool. If you get the names, call them!

In order to make this process as efficient as possible, ask your contact to call the selected individuals to let them know that you will be calling. Also ask him or her to tell them how important it is to have them call you back to make contact as soon as possible.

I have had a number of people who I was supposed to have talked to over the years put me on the bottom of the priority ladder. This was primarily because they didn't know who the hell I was. This was because my contact never let them know I would be calling. Don't let the same thing happen to you.

I've included a copy of the questionnaire I send out on the next page. Take mine and copy it if you want. Over time you may want to change it and customize it to your needs and make it even better.

Contracts for Speakers

You must use a contract every time you speak. Trust me, I have violated this rule and got severely burned.

If someone feels uncomfortable with signing a contract, you should probably not work with them.

Your contract should always require that a client give you 50% to hold a date. Do not mark a date as "booked" until the deposit has been received.

With your contract you have to be careful again not to be perceived as a prima donna. This is another area where you can make yourself look like a fool.

Unless you are a celebrity speaker, don't request first class airfare. Get them to pay for coach and upgrade yourself. Don't expect a client to pay for first class airfare. They probably don't travel first class and will be put off by these kinds of requests.

I've included a sample contract for you to peruse. I suggest you take a look at it and make any changes you feel appropriate. Then buy an hour of a lawyers' time and have them review it.

The Speaker as Consultant

Every speaker, by definition, is a consultant. By offering your services as a consultant, you will be much more likely to get consulting assignments from those organizations where you are or have been a speaker.

Get a hold of my book, "Consulting Secrets to Triple Your Income" to get a complete plan on how to make money as a consultant. Let me give you some of the basics here.

Very rarely will people pay you big money, sight unseen, to come in and do consulting for their organization.

People want to feel comfortable and confident with you before they start forking over their money.

This means that they will "enter your funnel" at various price points. Whenever anyone buys any service or product you provide, at any price point, they are entering your funnel. If you can get their name into your database you can start following up on them.

When they see you give a speech or seminar, many of those people have entered your funnel at zero cost to themselves. You then have to start trading them up your ladder to higher and higher priced products.

You will make them an offer during the speech or seminar for some of your products. Some will cost very little, others will be much more expensive. A certain number of people will buy from you. Your goal is to trade them up your ladder to more expensive products that you will produce. The most expensive product that you will offer is one-on-one consulting services.

So your key as a speaker is to develop a line of products, at a variety of price points. You must then work at trading them up the price ladder until you get to your highest end product, which is your consulting services.

Some clients will skip products on their way to using you as a consultant. I gave a speech a few years back. About 3 months later I got a call from a woman who was in the audience. She wanted me to come in and do consulting work in the marketing area. Did I turn her down? Of course not! But to think that this happens every day would be foolish, although you would hear stories like that one more frequently from those speakers and consultants who are well known: well published authors.

This happens infrequently. Usually, people have to buy at a lower price point, or a bunch of different price points before they feel comfortable making a larger, multi-thousand dollar a day consulting commitment.

As a speaker, you sell your knowledge in various forms. A speech or seminar is just one of them.

Consulting is another. Be sure to fill in the price gaps in between with various types of products.

One of the best ways to generate consulting business while giving a speech is to use this line no more than twice during your presentation, "In a recent meeting I had with one of my clients, I found ..." When you use this statement somewhere in your presentation, you are letting people know that you do consulting work. They most likely know this fact already, but you are subtly reinforcing it.

This is subtle if you only use this line once or twice; go beyond that and people will smell that what you're doing is an act. They will become less likely and not more likely to give you consulting work. You will be selling too hard.

The key to generating consulting business when you do seminars is to never withhold information. If you ever give people the feeling that you are not giving them all the "straight scoop", people will not respond well.

Some people think that if you keep a little bit of information in your back pocket, people will pay extra in order for you to show your cards. Nothing could be further from the truth. People are much more likely to give you consulting business when you give them everything you know and respond to all questions fully and forthrightly.

If you do this, people will be much more likely to ask you to come in and give them some individual help. No matter how much information you give out, they will still think you have more to give. When you hold back on information, you risk having them feel taken by some kind of a ruse to get you to give them more money. This is the wrong way to go.

The same thing holds true as it relates to product sales. When someone asks you a question and you respond with, "If you buy my tapes I go through all of that in more detail ... " you are dead in the water. People will feel rooked. You need to be 100% willing to give out any and everything you know during the hours of the seminar. You owe it to your participants. Give them this and they will give back to you in the form of major product sales.

Creating and Selling Your Information

Creating & Selling "Info" Products

First, let's define our terms. A product is any and everything you make available for sale before, during or after your speech or seminar, everything except your consulting services. These aren't products, but please sell these services as well!

It's important to understand that people learn using different modalities of learning. Some people like to read. For them we provide them with traditional books and ebooks. Others like to listen. For those folks we provide them with audios in form or cassettes and CD-roms. Still other people like to watch. Those people can be appealed to with DVDs and videos. Finally, there are people who like to experience. This group needs to be appealed to with seminars, teleseminars and bootcamps.

Take a look at the funnel system I've included on page 2. This will give you an accurate picture of what you need to do with people once you get them into your funnel. Assuming your goal as a speaker is to maximize revenue, you **must** create and sell products. A speaker who doesn't create and sell products is a fool. I have another book that you may want to pick up called "Selling Products from the Platform." If you want to learn even more about how to sell products from the platform, you need to read this. Check the back of this book for information on how to order.

Types of Products

Other than products you give away for free, the lowest price product you will most likely develop is a "special report." This is a 3 - 10 page report on a specific topic that you sell for less than $10.

Next on the list is your book. This will sell somewhere in the $10 – $30 range. There is a whole section about creating your book on page 51.

The next step-up in price would be your various length cassette programs. These will range in price from anywhere from $25 – $500 or even more. You will also see a great deal more products being produced on CD rom. The price range on these will be similar to those of your cassettes.

You'll probably want to offer a newsletter for somewhere in the $100 – $300 a year range.

Videos will generally go anywhere from $99 per video and up.

Disk products can be priced at anywhere from $39 to $500.

Additionally you'll be selling seats at your seminars and bootcamps. These will go for anywhere from $100 – $5,000. These aren't really products, but they are services you will offer. They are discussed in other sections of this book.

Outline the Product

In order to create any product, the first thing you will need to do is create a very extensive outline. This will be needed regardless of what form of product you choose to create.

Decide on the Medium

You'll also need to decide on whether you will produce a written, audio or video product. For years I preferred producing audio and video products. These are great and generally have higher price points but are less prestigious than a book. A report is obviously not as prestigious or lucrative.

Special Reports

A special report is a short concentrated report that gives people very specific information about a very narrow topic field.

Keep your special report to under 10 pages and pack it with information that can be immediately used and will provide your buyer with value.

Use a very direct approach and cut out all the war stories and other BS.

It is imperative that people who buy this report feel they have received exceptional value or they won't buy your next product or products.

Give people great information and a ton of resources they can investigate. Also, give them offers for additional products and services that you list at the end of the report. Remember: Upsell!

Audio Products

There are three basic ways to create audio products. The first way is to interview others and record the interviews. The second way is to record yourself and your own information. The third way is to create a script and go into a studio and record a product.

All of the audio programs you record will be able to be offered via the web. You will need to get them uploaded onto a server. When you get to that point, call me and I'll put you in touch with the right people to help you.

CREATING AUDIO PRODUCTS BY INTERVIEWING OTHERS

One of the quickest and easiest ways to create a product is to interview a guru in the field. If you wanted to put a product together on marketing, speaking or consulting, you could call me and interview me by phone. You could then take this interview and duplicate it onto tapes and sell these tapes for $20 or more. Hopefully more, if it's an interview with me! Ha.

Why would I or any other guru be willing to do this and not even charge you for it? Simple; we do it in exchange for you putting our contact information in numerous locations in that tape. That will allow me to further fill my funnel with leads at no cost to me other than the time I give you for the interview.

You must do the following, however, to make this type of scenario work.

■ Contact the person or persons you want to interview

■ Sell them on giving you the interview and letting you record it to fill their funnels for free.

I know that at least one speaker created a 12 cassette program entirely with interviews with experts. It took him less than a month to create and he sold the program for $295. All it took him to create this program was to spend 12 hours on the phone asking experts in a number of fields questions he wanted answered himself.

CREATING YOUR OWN AUDIO PRODUCTS

There are three ways to create your own audio products. The first is to record one of your own live seminars. The second way is to create an outline and go into a studio and go through a script rambling into a microphone. Third, you can ask a friend or colleague to interview you in a studio.

I use the studio term very loosely. You can create your own "studio" in a small room by padding the walls with material that will not allow the sound to bounce. The easiest thing to use is something like blankets.

LIVE RECORDING OF A SEMINAR

Take my suggestion and get a great audio recording device and microphone. Then take the recorder into your live seminar and record it, remembering to repeat all the questions you are asked.

I particularly like using this system when I have a small seminar around a table of six or eight people.

I will sometimes have a small seminar just to record the event. Never record a seminar that you haven't done at least eight or ten times. At that point in time, the material is new enough that you will sound enthusiastic, but you will still have done the seminar enough times to be pretty smooth and sound knowledgeable.

IN-STUDIO RECORDING

Sitting in a studio with an outline, trying to get excited talking to a microphone is one of the toughest ways to create a product. It can be done, but it's tough. My first few products were done this way. I don't think they are as good as my products that were recorded live or using the interview format.

The benefit is the amount of control you have over the process and finished product. Creating a product "in studio" gives you the greatest degree of control.

GET INTERVIEWED BY AN INTERVIEWER

I have a program called "How to Make $3,000 a Day as a Professional Speaker." It is one of my favorites because I used the interview technique. I had a friend named John Witty ask me the questions and I answered them.

We went through an outline that I created and gave to him the night before the seminar. He acted like the naive speaker who wanted to find out the information.

It worked because John is very quick-witted and has great improv skills. Quick on feet = good improv skills.

He is also a bright guy who had an interest in the topic. If you choose an interviewer, make sure they feel the same regarding your topic.

Whomever you choose, they should also have a good voice and pleasant manner. John fit the bill perfectly.

I like using the interview system to create products because people who listen to your program will often sit there listening and then feel like your interviewer asked exactly the question they wanted asked.

CASSETTE TAPES

I don't know how long they will be around, but cassette tapes continue to be the product of choice by speakers. They are cheap and easy to produce. Audio programs will be seen more and more on CD rom, but I don't see the audio cassette disappearing immediately.

At my office we have our own cassette tape duplicator. We do all of our small jobs of duplicating ourselves. It is much more cost effective.

EDITING

I would prefer you create programs that require no editing. Editing costs will eat you alive. Try to avoid it if at all possible. If you are worried about the occasional small mistakes you make on your audio programs, don't be. People will actually perceive you as more human.

CD Roms/Disk Products

Both CD Roms and disk products are items that I have done very little with myself at this point. I see that changing in the future.

In either of these cases, you will have to capture the information and then have it duplicated onto one of these two media. I don't see this as a big problem, but I have done very little work in this area.

Keep checking the web site: speakingformillions.com for more information in this area or call me at the office if and when you get to that point. I'll try to locate a source for you.

Video Products

One of the main reasons for producing and sell video products is because of their tremendous perception of value. People will pay a lot more for a video than they will for an audio or CD Rom. If you include a video or videos in your package of materials, you will also enhance the value of your packages.

LIVE RECORDING OF A SEMINAR OR EVENT

One possible way to create your video is to hire a crew to record a live event. This is tough to do, but when done right, can capture an energy you can't get from any other video form.

It requires doing a multi-camera shoot and will be fairly costly. If you consider doing this, make sure and contact me for some very important information and recommendations.

IN-STUDIO WITH A SCRIPT

You can take the presentation you normally do and go into a studio and replicate a live seminar. It will be OK if done correctly, but the energy will not be there. This isn't the wrong way to go, but it's certainly not the best way to do things. Others may do it, but I would highly recommend against it if at all possible.

IN-STUDIO WITH ACTORS

Producing videos using a script and actors is a difficult process. I have done close to a hundred "how to" videos over the years. When I first got started, I had no idea what I was doing.

The most important element is to have a good, well written script. The last thing you want to be doing is writing the script on the "set."

Unless you have a background in video production, I highly recommend that you get someone to help you. You may be able to get it done on your own, but you will be highly inefficient.

Duplicating Your Products

Duplicating audio tapes is easy. You can either do it yourself or send it out to a duplication house. Anything under 50 copies we do ourselves at the office. Anything over that amount we will normally send to a duplication house.

Check the resource section of this book as well the internet for vendors. I used to recommend a specific vendor named Dove. I can no longer recommend them. I now suggest you do most of your duplicating in-house. If you need to go to an outside vendor, give us a call at the office.

Packaging Your Products

As the last element in the product creation process before you start selling your products, you need to decide how you will package those products. You have some basic choices. Are you going to make them "fancy" or plain looking?

Before you think you know the answer, be careful not to get trapped in the "Nightingale-Conant Syndrome." They are one of the largest suppliers of learning audio tapes in the world. All of their packaging is done in 4 colors and looks very "sexy." The problem is that they price their products at around $10 to $15 per cassette.

By making your package look like theirs you will give people the impression that they should also sell for the same low prices. DON'T DO IT!

I suggest you package all of your products nicely, but simply. Use one color and don't try to compete with the "big guys." I do, however, offer a video or two with a full-color cover to make it look like I have something with a fancy package on it. Remember, people buy your content, not your packaging.

For all of your packaging needs I highly recommend Blackbourne and specifically Sylvia Tapelt. Tell her I told you to call. They sell any and all items for packaging including binders, cassette holder and the like.

Sell Your Products

You will want to sell all of your products that you create through every means possible. This will mean from the platform, through direct mail and through any and all other means possible.

Marketing Other Peoples Products

Just because you don't have your own products yet, doesn't mean you can't make money selling other peoples' products.

Before you have your own, you need to become a dealer for someone else's products. This way you can at least make <u>some</u> money rather than **no** money every time you speak.

You will naturally want to try to create your own as soon as possible, but don't miss out on making some money in the meantime.

Even after you create your own products, you may still want to sell other peoples' products if they are really good and don't compete with your own.

Find someone whose products you really like. Then approach them by explaining what you want to do. Most people will be willing to sell you their products at wholesale and let you sell them at retail.

Most people who will let you deal their materials will do so in one of two ways. They will either let you buy product from them directly and resell them, or they'll allow you to work a drop shipment deal with them.

Drop shipping has the advantage of your not having to pay to stock their inventory. You also won't have the hassle of shipping. The downside of this arrangement is that you will make less money.

The normal rates are the following. If you buy the products directly and stock them yourself, you will usually be able to get them at slightly over 50% off the retail price. If you set up a drop shipping arrangement, you will be able to get them at somewhere around 40% off the retail price.

Drop shipping will give you less money, but it is also less hassle. Other than cutting your margins, this customer is now HIS/HERS as well because they now have the customer's name and address and is in their database. This could potentially lose you money in the long run.

If you are interested in dealing some of my products, contact my office. The contact information is listed in both the front and back of this book.

Licensing

Licensing is a great way to create a cash flow surge and to get your name out into the market. I highly recommend that you license any and all products you create.

Here's how it works.

No matter what kind of product you create, you allow someone to buy a license. This gives someone the right to duplicate and sell your products at retail or whatever price point that they choose.

There are two basic types of licenses. First is the standard license.

With this license you give your licensees a master of whatever the product is. They can then duplicate these products at their cost and sell them to anyone they wish through any means. The only "proviso" is that they must keep the product intact and cannot make any changes to the product.

The cost of a standard license is usually ten to fifteen times your retail price for that product. For example, an audio tape program that I sell for $197 would have a licensing fee of between $2,000 and $3,000. The licensee would receive a complete set of masters along with any bonuses that go along with this product. They would also be given the right to duplicate any of the promotional material used to promote this product. This would include, but not be limited to, the sales letter and website used to market this product.

A MASTER license is an interesting concept. This arrangement gives the licensee the right to sell "standard" licenses to others. The price point for a master license is usually set at between forty and sixty times the retail price. The total in the above example is between $8,000 and $12,000.

It is a good idea to only sell a limited number of master licenses. Limit this number to a maximum of 20. A lesser number is probably even better. Too many master licenses will make it so that everyone will be trying to sell licenses. What will result is a mess! Depending on what market niche you're in you'll end up with a lot of master licensees trying to sell licenses to a limited number of people. This will be a problem and these folks will be annoyed with you. The greater the total number of potential licensees, the greater the number of master licenses you should sell.

If you sell too many master licenses you'll have a lot of people demanding their money back. In addition to that you'll have a low probability of being able to sell anything to them in the future.

The question is: why in your right mind would you sell people a license or a master license? Your other option would be to set people up as dealers or affiliates for the same products. In this type of arrangement people make 50% of the retail price. On a product priced at $197, they would make around $100.

From your standpoint, it would be better to keep people in this arrangement. YOU would make more money.

There are two main reasons to license your products. First, you get a cash flow surge. Second, your name and bounceback offers get out to a much larger number of people who you may not have been able to reach on your own. Since your licenses cannot change the product itself, all of your bouncebacks remain intact. Since most of your money is generated "on the back end", you have that many people getting your products into the market and into the hands of people who will end up in your funnel.

Selling Products from the Platform

Selling Products from the Platform

This section is a synopsis of another book that I have written called "Selling Products from the Platform." If after reading you would like more in depth information on this topic, please refer to the back of the book for ordering information. But this section will give you the basics you need to get started NOW.

Additional Prodding

Throughout the day, if you are working a full day seminar you can drop some subtle hints about your products. Don't do it too often, or you risk a backlash from your audience. If they feel you are over-selling, they will NOT buy. What is too frequent? I can't give you a specific number of instances, but as a rule of thumb, don't talk about your products more than once every two hours. And even then don't talk about them directly.

Description of Products and Specific Benefits

In order to sell your products, you must give people a reason for buying them. This happens as a result of giving them very specific benefits of each of your products. If you have a lot of products, you can go through these descriptions quickly, but make sure to stick to the major benefits your participants will derive from buying and using your materials.

Give a Great Presentation

The best way to sell a lot of products is to give a great presentation. Do this and people will naturally assume that your products are just as good. You should give your best effort every time you speak.

Three Tiered Pricing

When you sell products, try to give people an A, B, or C option. Take a certain number of products that you have and bundle them together. This will give you the ability to give people a low, medium and high priced offer Why do this? People need options. Give people choices and the question won't be if they will buy, but which they will buy.

Pricing Your Products

Many speakers tend to underprice their products. This is the biggest problem that most speakers have with products. The reason for this is the "Nightingale Conant Syndrome."

They are the largest provider of informational training materials on audio cassette in the world. They price their products on the very low end of the market. They tend to charge between $10 and $20 per cassette. Don't try to compete in this arena. Try to price your products at the high end and niche them to your various markets.

Create great products and price them at the high end of the spectrum. If you aren't comfortable charging a lot of money for your products, go back and redo them.

Be Confrontational of the Status Quo

You can't give people the standard material and content they have heard before from everyone else in the field if you want to move a lot of product. Your audience must feel that you are giving them new and different information, confrontational of the status quo if you are to be successful.

You Must be Liked/Respected by Your Audience

Unless your audience likes *and* respects you, the chances of getting them to buy products are slim to none. To get them to like and respect you, you need to answer questions fully and completely. You must also be careful to never make people feel less intelligent than you, either in your tone of voice or what you say to them.

Order Sheets

You should have your order sheets customized to each group you speak for. Have a special offer with their name at the top of the sheet. Give them an irresistible offer and you will sell a lot of product.

Hand out the order sheet right before the product presentation. I don't like the idea of having our participants seeing the order sheet until right before you do your pitch. This will keep them from spending time analyzing it before I have a chance to explain it.

Meet/Greet Before the Speech/Seminar

Many speakers act like big shots and arrive two seconds before they are announced. Audiences tend to buy more from those who are willing to mingle with the crowd, both before and after the event. You can appear like a rock star or you can make more money, but in this case, you can't have both. Schmooze people before your presentation and it will improve sales.

Order Today

Any offer you make for your products should give attendees a significant incentive to order on the spot. Whether you give them a significant price reduction or a collection of freebies, make them an incredible offer if they order right then and there.

Content Packed Seminar

Pack your speech or seminar with tons of great information and people will be much more apt to buy your products. The assumption that they will make is that if you packed your presentation with a plethora of meaty content, then your products will be the same.

Don't disappoint people by then selling them products that don't live up to expectations that you created when you spoke. Let them down in this area and risk a substantial amount of sales coming back as returns.

Checklist to Bring to Gigs

So as not to forget anything critical to your product sales efforts, put together a checklist of items to bring. Before you leave to go to an event, make sure you have everything on the list.

Once when I forgot one specific item that I usually bring, my sales were off by more than 20%. Don't make the same mistake.

Your Database of Seminar Attendees

Get all of your attendees' names and immediately have them input into a database. These names will be very valuable to you long term.

Those who have seen you in the past will be much more likely to buy your latest products or attend another event.

Measurement Eliminates Argument

The only way to tell how well you did with your product sales is through measurement. I use the same tool every time. I take the total amount of dollars sold and divide it by the total number of people in my audience.

So if I sold $10,000 worth of products and had 100 people in the audience, I have sold $100 per person. This gives me a very specific number to compare things to each and every time I speak.

Use this very objective measurement to determine your success at each event where you sell products.

Getting Association on Your Side to Sell Product

If you are speaking to an association audience, get them on your side to help push your products. The best way to do this is to give them a piece of the action.

I recently gave an association 15% of my product sales and they went nuts. They promoted the products so well that they made back a big portion of my speaking fee. I am 100% certain I will be back to speak to their group again.

Having Products in Inventory

People hate to spend money for anything they can't take with them today. Make sure you have sufficient product on hand to satisfy your anticipated demand.

It's better to have too much and have to ship some back than too little and risk losing some sales.

Over time you will figure out almost exactly how much product to bring. When in doubt, bring a little more than you think. The cost of shipping it back will be much less than the additional profits you'll lose by not having them immediately available.

Having Bags with Your Name on Them

I have canvas bags printed with the words, "Fred Gleeck's Marketing Magic System." This generic bag can be used in many different niche markets because all of my products are marketing related.

Having bags will serve as an ad for your products. Other people walking around at the event will see the bags and start asking questions to people who have them. This will help in your sales efforts.

Shipment of Product Owed

If you don't have enough product at the event, ship what you owe people immediately. They expect this and it will dramatically reduce your return rates.

Group Composition and Pricing

There are times when I have a group which I feel will not go for my normally high price points; then I will cut the numbers on the spot. How do I make this determination? It is based on "feel." Unfortunately, you'll only be able to get this feel after a considerable amount of practice. I'll take a package that normally sells for $495 and cut it to as low as $297 on certain rare occasions.

This can only be done after a great deal of practice or you'll lose money. There are times when I think I actually sell more when the price is high. Don't cut your profits unnecessarily by cutting your prices, but in some circumstances it may be the right move.

Product Shipment Errors/Other Problems

Clear up any product shipment errors quickly and include a small free gift. Once again, this will help build goodwill for your future sales efforts and reduce return rates.

What about Checks and Credit Cards?

You must offer both. Some people who sell products don't let their participants pay by check because they have been burned in the past. Don't do this. Take checks. A certain number will be bad but your net results will be positive. You'll get a lot more sales than not accepting them. This will more than pay for the bum checks you do get.

Most business people have one card they use exclusively for business. You must take credit cards or lose out on a lot of product sales.

Payment Terms

You should be testing the idea of offering people payment terms. See what will happen if you give people the option to pay in three installments.

I also have talked to a famous marketing guru who told me to test giving people the products and not billing their credit cards for a full month. He said that this would increase my sales but also increase my refund rate.

His guess is that the increase in sales would far exceed the increase in refunds. As I write this section of the book I have still not tested this concept. Keep in touch to hear the latest on this and other ideas.

Upselling at the Product Table

When people come to your product table ready to buy, this is the best time to bump up your sale. Have a special offer good for that day and time only.

Tell people that if they buy today they can get an additional program that normally sells for $99 for just $33. Ask them if they would like to add that to their order.

If it has a great title, you will sell a bunch of them. Also, you will still be making an additional $25 in profit because your cost will be somewhere around $8 for the item.

Tape All Your Product Presentations

In order to make the most money selling products you need to record every presentation. When something happens one day and you sell twice as much as usual, you'll want to review that tape, transcribe it, and figure out what worked so well.

If you don't have it on tape, you will spend the next five years trying to figure out what you did right. Trust me, it hurts. Tape everything!

Your Own vs. Other People's Products

Don't forget that you can make money selling other peoples' products as well. If you are just starting out, or even if you're not, if there are some products you really love and can support, become a dealer for those products.

Some people find it much easier to "hawk" other peoples' stuff than their own. As you develop great products, this should be much less difficult for you, but in the meantime go ahead and get yourself set up to deal other peoples' products. I have numerous dealers for a variety of my products.

Generic vs. Specific Products

You will have infinitely greater success if your products are targeted to the specific groups you speak to rather than offering a number of general products.

People will feel that, if your products are targeted specifically to them and their niche, they will be worth buying and will be worth far more money. You can therefore ask for more money as a result.

Continual Mailers

Your product sales effort continues even after you have left the event. You need to follow up with your attendees in writing after the event. The best way is with a series of mailers to those who didn't buy trying to get them to buy something, however small or inexpensive.

Also, follow up on those who did buy by trying to upsell them to additional products or services that are more lucrative for you and more helpful to them.

Mental Preparation

You have to be in the right mental state to sell a lot of products. Those events where I have been in a great, highly positive mood, inevitably netted me much better numbers in product sales.

Find out what you need to do before each presentation to put yourself, even artificially, into this mental state.

Look/Dress

From a product sales perspective, the only way to deal with what you will wear is to test different modes and see what ends up giving you the best results.

There is no way that I can give you a suggestion on what will work best because it will vary from person to person. Write down what you wear at each presentation and then see what the numbers tell you.

It's Not Your Fault — There is a Better Way

To maximize product sales, it's important that when people attend a presentation of yours that you never make them feel like their shortcomings are their fault. You should show them how their circumstances have put them into that situation.

You then illustrate to them how your presentation and more importantly, your products will help them find the better way.

100% Absolute Confidence in Your Products

Unless you have 100% confidence in your products, the chances of your product sales figures being very good are slim.

If you are not fully confident with your materials, go back and redo them until you can feel fully confident in their being able to help your buyers. Without truly feeling this way about your own products, the chances of selling them to anyone are slim to none.

Guarantee

A strong, powerful guarantee is critical to product sales success. I tell people that unless they make 10 times what they paid for my products over the course of the next year, they should send them all back.

In one of my markets I offer people a lifetime guarantee. The minimum guarantee length I would suggest is a year. Anything less than that amount will make people concerned about the quality and content of your products.

The Transition and Start of the Pitch

When I was doing seminar work for CareerTrack, they made me deliver the pitch using a transition that made it look like the pitch was part of the content presentation.

No matter how good you are as a speaker, this technique is totally transparent. People know when you are selling. Don't try to disguise it by designing some kind of transition to try to fool people into thinking you are still delivering content.

People will greatly appreciate the direct and straight-forward sales approach.

The Action Idea Sheet

In every seminar, use the Action Idea Sheet as discussed in a different section of the book. This will help show people how much content you gave them.

When you illustrate that you deliver a lot of content in the seminar, they will expect to receive a similar amount of content in your products.

Displaying Your Products

People should be able to see your products displayed before your presentation begins. You want to have them sitting around for people to take a look at. Don't make your display look too much like an obvious sales effort. The more casual your approach to the display, the better. I like to have a more formal display up towards the front of the room where people will be looking while I speak. I don't make any mention of the products until I start my pitch.

Timing of the Product Pitch

You can't pitch your products until you have built rapport and gained the confidence of your audience. With a one hour presentation, don't pitch any earlier than at the 48 minute point. With a three hour presentation and longer, pitch no earlier than half way through the presentation.

Answer all Questions Fully and Completely

A big mistake that some speakers make when selling products is not to answers all the questions they get asked fully and completely.

The result of doing things that way will be that people will feel that you have short changed them. They expect you to give them all of your information during the time that you are supposed to be speaking to them.

Many speakers feel that, if they hold back and don't fully answer questions asked from the audience, they will sell more product. Nothing could be further from the truth. I think this is because they will feel a lot more comfortable and confident buying your products if they see how willing you are to answer questions during your allotted time together.

Participants will infer that you will be equally willing to reveal the most important information on your tapes and other materials and will be more apt to buy.

Go Quickly, Leave People a Little Overwhelmed, a Tad Confused, Yet Favorably Impressed

I speak at a New Yorker's pace. This is because I spent so much time in that city, but it is also a very intentional technique on my part.

Speaking quickly will give people the impression (true or not) that you have a plethora of material to cover, but won't get through it all unless you move quickly. This will make participants feel like there is so much more for you to give them.

The net result will be an increase in your product sales. This will make them much more likely to buy more.

I Don't Need the Money,
But You Can't Afford Not to Have the Product

If your audience gets the feeling that you must make a sale to them in order to pay your bills this month, your chances of making a sale are very slim.

You need to make your audience feel that they will benefit a lot more than you will as a result of purchasing any of your materials.

Also critical to your sales effort is building value of your products through your benefit laden descriptions. This should leave them with the feeling that they will be much worse off if they don't shell out the money and buy your materials.

Internet Strategies for Speakers

Speaker Internet Strategies

No book can be written without talking about how you can market your business on the internet. This book and the speaking business are no different.

I see the internet as most effective when used as a lead generating device. You can generate leads either through your own web site or a variety of existing sites that are geared to promoting you as a speaker and your events as a seminar leader.

I also think that as a speaker you should "surf the net" to see what is going on in the marketplace. Things are changing so quickly that you need to keep a finger on the pulse of the market. This is easiest done on-line.

Your Own Website

The first thing you need is your own site. I would suggest that you make it "your name.com." I have fredgleeck.com. Your site should have a link on your first page that will immediately take them to a description of your speaking services and offerings.

The place where you should go to set up your domain name is "000domains.com." This will let you set up your domain name for $13.50 a year. This is the cheapest I have found anywhere on the web. If you find something cheaper, please let me know.

Once you set up your domain name, you will have to find a place to "park" your site. To get started, I highly recommend that you use wizmo.com. This is a very basic free website which has a number of templates that you can choose from. They also have toll free customer support. This is amazing for a free website. These folks know what they are doing and I highly recommend them.

After your speaking career is further along (or if you are there already), you will probably want to develop a more sophisticated site. This would include audio and video clips of you as a speaker. Check the website (speakingformillions.com) for the latest information regarding vendors.

I took it upon myself to learn how to use a basic web design program called Pagemill from Adobe Systems. I hate being at the mercy of the web design community. I was treated very badly early on by a number of unscrupulous operators so I wanted to understand how to do it myself. A waste of my time? Perhaps, but I feel more comfortable doing it this way.

Sites That Can Help You as a Speaker

There are a number of sites out there that can help you as a speaker. As these are changing constantly, I suggest you check "speakingformillions.com" for the latest websites that can help you as a speaker.

Surfing the Net

I want to give you an obvious recommendation. Like I mentioned earlier, you should search the web on a regular basis and put in the word "speaker" and "seminar leader." This will keep you informed about the latest developments in the field as it relates to speakers.

You will be able to find any of the new opportunities as soon as they present themselves.

Other Helpful Speaking Info

Travel Suggestions for the Speaker

This may seem like a frivolous chapter. Once you start speaking actively, trust me, you won't think so.

Once you start working regularly as a professional speaker, you will be amazed at how much of an issue travel will become. There is nothing worse than having a bad travel experience, arriving at your hotel at 2AM and then having to get up at 6 AM to do an all day seminar.

All of a sudden, you will become very aware of airline, hotel, and rental car companies and policies.

You will be amazed at how important all of these things will become. You will realize why speakers are obsessed about frequent flyer miles and why they always rent cars from the same company.

Airlines

Selecting the right airline and getting in with the right frequent flier program is the most important of all of your travel elements. If you travel a lot with one airline like I do you will be able to upgrade for minimal (and sometimes no) fees.

Airline Clubs

You must have a membership at least one airline travel club, at preferably one which has reciprocal privileges with an airline that has a large international presence. The reason for this is because you will have to use your time productively between flights. It is a lot better than sitting in the general waiting areas provided by the airport.

These memberships will cost you between $200 and $400 a year and are worth every penny that you spend on them if you are traveling a lot as a speaker.

Luggage

You need to have good luggage as a speaker. When I first started in the business I bought some basic, relatively cheap luggage. Take it from me, buy good luggage and you won't have to buy it more than once.

My recommendation is that you buy the Travel Pro Platinum Series luggage. This isn't the best luggage on the market, but it is pretty damn good and has a lifetime guarantee. Whatever brand name you decide on, they MUST have a lifetime guarantee.

You will need at least three different sizes of luggage to have sitting around. I have one piece that is a carry-on size that allows my brief-case to attach to it. It is small enough to comply with all the size regulations of even the most conservative airline. This way there is no situation in which I am forced to check it.

I then get a slightly larger piece for trips of slightly longer duration. Again, make sure that this one has wheels also. It should also allow you to attach other pieces to it to make it easy to transport them.

I also have two different size garment bags, one for a quick overnight trip and one for any longer length trip that demands I take suits along with me.

Rental Cars

Get a relationship going with one rental car company. Make sure it is one of the major ones. They will have lots of airport locations and all of them will be connected to one or all of the major frequent flier programs.

The reason you want to do this is that you will have a lot more clout with that company. They will give you special "status" as one of their elite members. Avis calls it a "preferred" renter. This will allow you various perks, like upgrades and not having to go inside to check the car out when you get to the parking lot.

I would recommend that you go with Avis, but any of the major companies will give you similar perks and privileges.

Hotels

I try to always use hotels that are connected to my frequent flier program if my client is paying. Whichever frequent flier program you decide on, get a list of which hotel chains they are affiliated with and try to use only those hotels whenever possible.

When I can't use one of these hotels I always stay at a Hampton Inn. I prefer them over and above all the well known name brands that have supposedly better reputations. They do a great job and understand customer service.

Packing

I am a terrible packer. I always tend to take more than what I need. Get a hold of a book on packing if you don't know how to do it. It will save you time, money and aggravation.

Remember to always have the essential elements of your speech or seminar "on your person" whenever you are traveling. Not that I am suggesting that the airlines tend to lose luggage a lot or anything!

Getting Books at Below Cost or Free

As a speaker and product seller, there is a legitimate way for you to get books at below cost or even free. Why do you deserve this? Because it is possible that you may want to consider selling some of these books at your seminars or speeches, it is perfectly legitimate that you are allowed to preview books from the various publishing houses.

In addition to seeing whether or not you will sell these books that you preview at your events, you will also be able to keep up to date on various topics in your field. Your research in your topic area becomes much easier when you can get books in your field sent directly to you for free.

Here is how to do it.

First you need to contact each of the individual publishing houses. You will generally want to speak to someone who is in the "special sales" department. This is the area where they try to sell books through non-traditional channels. You will generally speak to a 20-something "kid" who sends out review copies after explaining the request to their boss.

Your key to making this happen is to let them know that you have the potential to sell a lot of books through non-traditional channels. This would include back of the room sales at seminars, as well as through direct mail to your database. The larger the database you have or claim to have, the more impressed the publishing houses will be.

Pitching the "kid" will be an indirect sales effort. You have to sell them on selling their boss.

They will usually ask you to send them some of your promotional materials to show that you are legitimate. Send them whatever they request. It will help you get what you want.

If you've done a good sales job, the special sales department will ask you which topics you want to preview. Don't be too demanding. Ask for no more than four or five books at a time. This request will usually be honored.

Very soon thereafter, you will get your free books in the mail.

Getting Your Printing Done

As a speaker and seminar leader you will inevitably need to get things printed. Be careful, this is an area where speakers get royally screwed all the time.

There are huge variations of prices on printing. I recently priced a job and the highest price was over 300% of what my lowest price was for the exact same job.

Make sure to get a minimum of three quotes for any decent size printing job that you do. It will be a lot more difficult for you to get taken advantage of if you do it that way.

Take a look on-line at a place called americasprinter.com.

Critiquing Yourself and Others

Most speakers have fragile egos. They hate to hear anything other than praise about a speech that they gave. I love to hear criticism. I don't take all of it seriously, but I do listen to all of it.

I think my limited acting background taught me one very critical lesson. A director will very seldom be happy with how you do a scene the first time. In fact, even if they like what you did, they will ask you to try it another way to see if you can make it even better.

If you don't listen to criticism, you will never improve. The problem is two fold. First, you need to never take it personally. This is easy to say and tough to do.

Second, you need to evaluate the source of the criticism. Is the person giving you the criticism someone you respect? Do they have the requisite knowledge to give you a valid critique? If the answer to either of these questions is no, listen to what they say, but ignore it.

There is also another problem. When I give a speech, I have a very specific yardstick with which I measure my speaking success at a given event. It has to do with two very quantifiable things. First are my evaluations. How much did people say they liked what I did?

Second are my product sales numbers. This should really be the first item I mentioned. If I do well in the product sales area, it is telling me I did a good job speaking. If not, people wouldn't buy my products.

What about giving criticism to other speakers? The first thing to remember is this. Many of them will say they want to hear it. In reality, they don't. Most speakers have incredibly fragile egos. Say anything negative about their speaking ability and they will fall apart. Maybe not on the outside, but on the inside.

My suggestion? Don't give out any unsolicited criticism to another speaker. From a highly competitive stand point, all you are doing is helping them improve. And they are your competition. Also, they really don't want it.

What about when people ask for criticism? Over the years I have coached hundreds of speakers. I always let them know in advance that I am the wrong coach if they are looking for someone to pat them on the head every time they speak and tell them what a good job they did.

Before I give speakers an answer to the question: "What did you think of my speech?" I always ask them if they want the truth, or if they want me to make them feel good. Usually they are shocked by the question. The reason is that the 'fraternity" of speakers are very wary of actually giving out a truthful assessment in this area. They would rather just say to each other: "You were great."

That kind of a comment never helps an actor give a better performance and will <u>never</u> help a speaker improve.

I love getting critiques from my audience. If they don't buy at least $100 per person, then I know I haven't given them sufficient value in my presentation.

My suggestion is to listen to criticism from other speakers you respect. But most of all, listen to your audience. They are the people who matter the most.

Names of Speakers Worth Hearing

I wanted to give you a list of speakers, who I consider worth hearing. These in addition to myself, of course!

Let me warn you in advance that some of the speakers who categorize themselves as professionals are awful. I saw a speaker not long ago who is the author of a well known book on customer service. For a one hour speech he had prepared a six page, single spaced handout. ABSURD!

When you see a speaker you like, ask yourself what it was about them that you found so appealing. Using this critical eye when you watch others will help you to critique yourself.

While watching, concentrate on the two major elements of speaking: style and content. You will find some speakers are masters of delivery but are very light on substance. After you listen to them, it's very much like eating Chinese food where you seem to be hungry again (for information) soon after.

Others you will find have great content but are impossible to tolerate because of their poor delivery. Understand that you need both to move into the top tier of speaking professionals.

Let me give you a list of speakers to look out for; if they are in your area, go see them.

First there is Lou Heckler, in my opinion, one of the greatest speakers ever. Note how he uses humor. Also notice that he is the epitome of a "what you see is what you get" speaker. There is not a fake bone in this man's body. Just seeing him speak will make you better.

Just like with movies, you have to see some of the classics. Zig Ziglar would be one of those. You can form your own opinions about Zig, but he has been a speaking classic for nearly a half century.

Brian Tracy is another speaker to hear. Pay particular attention to how much content Brian can put into a presentation. This guy is nearly all meat and no fat. Learn from what he does.

It's always a good idea to see what might be called today's hot choice. That would be someone like Tony (Anthony) Robbins. This guy gets paid really big money for a presentation. Try to see if you can figure out why.

That's a pretty good list. If one of the Peter Lowe Success Events comes to your city, try to go. It's a long day, but you'll hear a lot of speakers who you can learn from. You may wonder why some of them are there. Don't worry. I felt the same way.

Are there other speakers I haven't mentioned who are worth seeing? Probably, but not that many.

Selecting a Mentor

In any business, speaking included, it is always nice to have someone show you the ropes from the inside. Speaking is no exception.

A mentor will speed up the rate at which you learn the speaking business.

How do you find a mentor? There is no one specific way. I don't recommend that you walk up to a speaker and say: "Wanna be my mentor?" This will not work. Most speakers will hand you a card and ask you to call their office to set up some consulting time, for a fee.

The essence of finding a suitable mentor has to do first and foremost with mutual respect. The accomplished speaker must respect you as a person as much as you respect their knowledge and ability as a speaker.

A mentor need not be someone you talk to every day or even every week. It is someone who will take your call, or call you back quickly when you call them.

People have mentors at different levels of involvement. I always wanted a mentor who would never feel like I was being a pain in their a _ _. This means that I called them infrequently. I always respected their time. I always thanked them on the phone and with a follow-up note or letter.

I listened to their suggestions, I did what they told me to do, and I reported back to them on what happened as a result.

The biggest issue on mentor compatibility has to do with personality and disposition. Basically, you need someone you get along with.

I approached my chosen mentor soon after he finished a speech. I introduced myself and I then followed up in a non-pushy way. I sent him small gifts and endeared myself to him and his wife. This proved to be a good approach.

I don't think there is one way to find or select a mentor. But I will warn you, speakers are busy people. Be respectful of their time. Try to make them feel like you aren't being a pest.

Seminars All Speakers Should Attend

I am a very critical seminar attendee. Having done over 3,000 seminars (that number may actually be higher but I've lost count) over my years in the business, I hate wasting my own time.

I frankly find the vast majority of seminars to be packed with fluff and severely lacking in substance.

Over the years I have found a few that I would like to recommend to you. They helped me immensely and I'm sure they will have the same effect on you. No one who I have recommended attend these seminars has ever come back with anything other than very positive comments.

First, you need to come to any and all of my events. I am the only one that I know of that has a lifetime money back guarantee on any and all speaking related events I promote. How can I do this? Because the seminars deliver what is promised. If they don't, you don't pay. It's that simple. Check the website for more information on upcoming events.

Go to a seminar that Robert Pike teaches on "Creative Training Techniques." His origination offers a number of different courses, but this is the only one I would recommend.

It will teach you numerous ways to make your seminars and speeches more interesting. Get them to send you a brochure. It is a two day seminar and is worth whatever price they are charging for it these days. I took it a number of years back when it cost $495. I think it is up around $795 these days. It is still worth every penny. Call them at 1-800-383-9210.

Everything I have ever taken offered by the Franklin Covey organization has been good. They deliver strong content with very good speakers. Take their course on time management. It's excellent. They can be reached at 1-800-487-1847.

Continual Learning

I regularly listen to audio tapes and attend many seminars. I love to learn and I expect to get what I pay for. I suspect you are probably the same.

Last year I spent well over $10,000 on seminars, audio tapes, and other learning tools for myself. I consider this a worthwhile investment.

If you feel the same way I do, always find out what the guarantee is before you buy anything. Unless they have an iron clad money back guarantee, don't buy it, no matter what it is.

If I'm not happy, I will ask for my money back. Do not buy anything from anyone unless they offer you a money back guarantee. If they don't offer this guarantee, then ask them why not.

It is always interesting to hear what they say.

The Future of Speaking and YOUR Future

Future Speaking Trends

What does the future hold for the speaking business? Here are some of my ideas.

■ Teleconferencing and connections on the internet will not eliminate the need for speakers. I hear speakers talking all the time about how technology will put them out of a job. I completely disagree. The greater the advances in technology, the greater the need will be for real live human contact. Speakers qualify in this category.

■ The internet will virtually eliminate the need for speaker promotional materials and thus cut speaker cost and lower overhead.

■ Strictly motivational speakers will be less and less in demand. Successful speakers will need to have plenty of good content.

■ The most successful speakers will be those who are primarily in the business of promoting their own events.

■ Product revenue will become a larger and larger portion of successful speakers' revenues.

■ Speakers who are poor marketers will have a hard time making a real living, regardless of their speaking skills.

■ Presentations which are primarily based on the use of sexy technology will fall victim to those speakers who have great fundamental speaking skills.

■ Bureaus will become less of an issue as speakers find more and more ways to connect directly with those organizations and individuals who need speakers.

Your Personal System for Success

You're done reading the book. You have all the information you need to succeed. Now you need a specific plan to make things happen. Without a plan, your chances of making yourself a success as a speaker are virtually impossible. The key to success in speaking is simple. You have to be a great speaker and a tremendous marketer.

To be a superb speaker you need to have an abundance of great content and a great speaking style. These items you can work on. Very few people start out as natural public speakers.

To be a great marketer, you have to do whatever is necessary to succeed. Do everything that I tell you in this book. You will find that you enjoy certain kinds of marketing more than others. Fine. Concentrate on them.

There is no general system for success for every speaker. Your plan will be different from mine because of your area of expertise and your marketing skills.

Here is a checklist of items to jump start your speaking career.

- How will you get famous?
- What audio product will you produce in the next 30 days?
- Where can you speak for free to practice?
- What topic or topics will you speak on?
- Where will you get some articles published?
- When will you write your book?
- What system will you design for following up on leads?
- Which bureaus will you contact?
- Attend seminars and conferences to advance your speaking and marketing skills.
- Start doing research: check to see if method is acceptable.
- Set up files on stories, quotes and humor.

These are just a few, but you need to get started. So get going now!

What You Need to Do to Get Started NOW!

1. Start Speaking

There are waiters who call themselves actors in New York City. The reason is that some of them will not take certain types of acting jobs. It is beneath them. Take any speaking engagement you can get., no matter how small or insignificant. If you claim to be a speaker, you have to be speaking. Speak anytime, anywhere, even if it's for free. You must, of course, be allowed to sell your products.

2. Start Writing

Start getting articles published for your press kit. This will immediately increase your credibility and make it easier for you to get booked as a speaker. Don't try to land the big, well-known publications. Start with the smaller niche magazines. Make sure that you have a bounceback offer for your website autoresponder.

3. Start Creating Your Promotional Materials

Go through the section of the book and create all of the basic promotional material. As a minimum you need to have your one page faxable data sheet about yourself, plus basic web site for yourself, your products and your speaking services.

4. Develop Some Products

Create some inexpensive products immediately. This way, when you start speaking for free, you will at least be able to generate a few dollars from the sales of your product or products. Even if it's just one audio tape, get it out there.

5. Write Your Book

My biggest mistake was not writing a book earlier. Don't make this mistake. Take the topic you are most passionate about and most want to speak about and start writing your book. The faster you get this done, the faster your speaking career will take off. Get my book called: "Self Publishing For Maximum Profit."

6. Generate Publicity for Yourself

Look for any available opportunity to get yourself in the media. This should be done with the intention of generating names for your database. Do at least one thing everyday that will get you in front of the media. It should be like brushing your teeth.

7. Learn from Others

Watch other speakers. Go to speaking events. If you have the opportunity, attend one of my seminars for beginning speakers. You can't learn enough in the beginning. Be a sponge for any and all information. Read all the books I have listed in the resource section. But remember to beware of the "sharks."

The 7 Biggest Mistakes Speakers Make

1. Not Specializing in a Niche/Niches

You must pick niches to specialize in. It is better for you to build deep, than wide. Pick one market and exploit it to the hilt. Only after you have fully entrenched yourself in a niche and produced a ton of products should you consider moving to the next.

2. Not Producing Products

Speakers who don't have an extensive line of products will make a lot less money than those who do. If money isn't important to you, then don't produce any products.

3. Not Concentrating on Marketing

No matter how great a speaker you are, marketing is critical. Concentrate on your speaking skills and your content, but remember, without a strong marketing plan, no one will ever hear you.

4. Not Writing a book

Speakers who write books make more money and make it to the top faster than those who don't. Don't just sit there reading this — START WRITING!

5. Concentrating on Fluff, not Meat

I don't care how good your skills as an orator are, if you don't deliver solid and useable information, you won't be successful as a speaker. Give people information that is solid and easy to use.

6. Not Delivering on Your Promises

If you tell people how great you are and don't deliver on your promises, your speaking life will be very short. Don't make promises you can't keep. Deliver more value than people expect.

7. Not Keeping a Great Database

A key to your speaking success will be repeat business, both in terms of speaking engagements and product sales. Keep every name of every person who hears you speak or buys your products on a database. Mail to them at least 4 times a year. That is an absolute minimum.

FREE SPEAKING TIPS:

To receive regular tips on how to start and build a successful speaking business send an email to:

tips@professionalspeakingsuccess.com.

Conclusion

If you're like me, you are reading this chapter having not yet read every page in this book. That's fine. There may be certain areas that are not immediately interesting or relevant to you.

You now have to make a big decision. What are you going to do with this new information? Are you going to sit around and think about things? Please don't.

When I first read a book on speaking, it took me over five years to finally act on the information. Looking back on this decision, I can only tell you that it was a big mistake, not just because of the money, but because of the time that I lost.

Time lost doing things I didn't enjoy. I could have been doing what I have found I really love — SPEAKING.

I can't reach out and grab you physically, but I can leave you with this:

If you really love to speak and think you could do it fairly well, get started. Don't wait until things slow down. Don't wait until the time

---

is right. Don't wait until "someday." That someday is **now** and I sincerely believe that there was a reason why you found this book.

If you need my help, call me! I have helped many hundreds of people get their speaking careers on track.

There is nothing more satisfying for me than to see people do great things and for me to be even partially responsible for their success. Forget the money. This makes me feel great.

It will make you feel even greater if you take my suggestion and get started. Now put this book down and do something, something that will get you on the road to doing what you know you want to do.

You have the blueprint to succeed in your hands. You need nothing else but to decide to do it. So do it. And get on the road to ...

Becoming a professional speaker!

Million-Dollar Rolodex

Fred Gleeck's Key Contacts for you to call. Always use my name!

Contact Management (Database) Software - ACT! from Symantec 800-441-7234; www. symantec.com

Accountant: 212-628-3139, Chris Trinka

Incorporation/Attorney: Steve Soden; Soden and Steinberger 619-239-3200

Copywriter: 925-254-1926, Alex Mandossian, ohanalex@home.com

Editor: Bronwen Brown, 212-987-2487

Search Engine Optimization: Kimberly Judd, kjudd@cybermarkint.com

Website Registration: www.godaddy.com ($8.95/year for dot.com, .net, .org.)

Computer Hardware/Software: Macwarehouse/Microwarehouse 800-622-6222

Cassette Tapes/Duplicating Machines - Kingdom - 800-788-1122

Deborah Data: Data Entry work (from cards of directories); about 21¢ each entry; 888-420-3282

Audio/Video/CD Duplication: www.duplicationdepot.com - 800-950-0608 (ask for Gary Brown)

Cassette Packaging: Blackbourne: 888-676-6773 (Sylvia Tapelt)

Telephone Bridge Lines: telephonebridgesavers.com: 800-345-3325

Website Design/Webhosting Services: at
webproblemsolver@aol.com; 212-240-1903 (Darrell Boyce)

Transcription Services - VERBATIMIT.com - 802-864-5696
(ask for Alan Kelly)

Book cover and interior design: Tamara Dever,
TLC Graphics, www.tlcgraphics.com, tamara@tlcgraphics.com

BookSurge; Book printing, sales, distribution:
www.booksurge.com, 866-308-6235 (John Barker)

Franklin Covey Group: 800-487-1847
(Time Management Seminars)

Robert Pike: Creative Training Techniques: 800-383-9210
(Take ONLY this seminar from them)

Credit Card Merchant Accounts: e-commerce exchange:
800-675-6573

Wall Calendar/Smart Chart (for your speaking office to keep
your schedule) 800-872-0232

Viking Office Products 800-421-1222

American Society for Training and Development:
www.ASTD.org; 800-628-2783

National Speakers Association: nsaspeaker.org; 480-968-2552

Website References:

www.webmarketingmagic.com: system for automating
your process as a speaker

www.seminarexpert.com: for those speakers interested in seminar marketing

www.radiopublicity.com: learn how to generate radio interviews

www.telephonebridgsavers.com: the site for setting up
teleconference lines

www.consultingexpert.com: the site for those speakers interested in doing consulting work

www.speeking.com: for those interested in professional speaking

Miscellaneous Important Organizations

Associations to Consider Joining:

Toastmasters International
P.O. Box 9052
Mission Viejo, CA 92690
(714) 858-8255

American Society for Training and Development
1630 Duke St., P.O. Box 1443
Alexandria, VA 22313
(703) 683-8100

National Speakers Association
1500 South Priest Drive
Tempe, AZ 85281
480-968-2552 – phone
480-968-0991 – fax
nsaspeaker.com

Direct Marketing Association
6 East 43rd Street
New York, NY 10017-4646
(212) 768-7277

Public Seminar Companies:

American Management Association: (212) 586-8100

Dunn & Bradstreet Seminars: (800) 234-3867

Keye Productivity Center and Padgett Thompson Seminars (800) 255-4141

Speakers Bureau List:

(Some of these will not be appropriate for all speakers)

Barnes Curci Marketing
15510 Rockfield, Suite C
Irvine, CA 92718
949-768-2942 - phone
949-768-0630 - fax

Billy Mills Speakers Bureau
7760 Winding Way, Suite 722
Fair Oaks, CA 95628
916-965-5738 - phone
916-965-9317 - fax
millsgold@aol.com

Blanchard Speakers Bureau
125 State Place
Escondido, CA 92029
760-489-5005- phone
760-233-3657 - fax

Convention Connection
18133 Coastline Drive #3
Malibu, CA 90265
310-459-0159- phone
310-454-2518 - fax
suzanne@speakersrus.com

DE Associates
174 Harvard Drive
Larkspur, CA 94939
415-924-1469- phone
800-332-3618
415-927-3047 - fax
derick1469@aol.com

Excellence in Presentations
11129 Walmort Road
Wilton, CA 95693
916-687-8486- phone
800-345-1758
916-687-8486 - fax
eip-tommunter@juno.com
www.tpw.com/ca/eip

Fisher Group/Jostens Speakers
Bureau
P.O. Box 727
Danville, CA 94526
925-831-1229 - phone
925-820-6371 - fax
jostenssb@aol.com
www.jostensSpeakersBureau.com

Great Speakers!
359 North Oak Street
Ukiah, CA 95482
707-463-1081 - phone
707-463-1088 - fax
info@greatspeakers.com

Irv Bernstein & Associates, Inc.
7660 Fay Avenue, Suite 278-H
La Jolla, CA 92037
619-459-8553 - phone
619-459-8580 - fax
ibasnet@san.rr.com
www.ibaspeakernet.com

Key Speakers Bureau, Inc.
3500 E. Coast Highway, #6
Corona Del Mar, CA 92625
949-675-7856 - phone
949-675-1478 - fax
canada@keyspeakers.com
www.keyspeakers.com

Keynote Speakers, Inc.
425 Sherman Avenue, Suite 200
Palo Alto, CA 94306
650-325-8711 - phone
650-325-8737 - fax
barbara@keynotespeakers.com

Lectures International
P.O. Box 180830
Coronado, CA 92178
619-423-3076 - phone
800-219-6983 - fax
lectintl@worldnet.att.net

Santa Barbara Speakers Bureau
145 Canon Drive
Santa Barbara, CA 93105
805-682-7474 - phone
805-563-1028 - fax
Michael@speakingpros.com
www.speakingpros.com

Speakers Bureau Unlimited
24195 Juanita Drive
P.O. Box 3116
Quail Valley, CA 92587
909-244-1885 - phone
909-244-5466 - fax
lilly@cdlilly.com
www.cdlilly.com

Speakers Source
18425 Burbank Boulevard #706
Tarzana, CA 91356
818-776-1244 - phone
818-776-1174 - fax
speaker@robbinsgrp.com

Standing Ovations
8380 Miramar Mall #107-109
San Diego, CA   92121
858-455-1850 - phone
858-455-1576 - fax
nanpratt@earthlink.net

Strictly Speakers
73-255 El Paseo, Suite 19
Palm Desert, CA   92260
760-340-1652 - phone
760-773-3636 - fax
pgribow@strictlyspeakers.com
www.strictlyspeakers.com

The Aviation Speakers Bureau
P.O. Box 6030
San Clemente, CA   92674
949-498-2498 - phone
800-247-1215
www.aviationspeakers.com

World Class Speakers &
Entertainers
10747 Wilshire Blvd., Suite 807
Los Angeles, CA   90024-4432
310-441-7229 - phone
310-441-7233 - fax
info@speak.com
www.speak.com

Gold Stars Speakers Bureau
P.O. Box 37106
Tucson, AZ   85740
520-742-4384 - phone
520-797-3557 - fax
info@goldstars.com
www.goldstars.com

Brooks International Speakers
Bureau
763 Santa Fe Drive
Denver, CO   80204

303-825-8700 - phone
303-825-8701 - fax
maureen@brooksinternational.com
www.brooksinternational.com

National Academic Speakers
Bureau, Inc.
P.O. Box 216
Storrs, CT   06268
860-486-2454 - phone
860-486-0641 - fax
info@ogbar.com

The Goodman Speakers Bureau,
Inc.
6 Poquonock Avenue, Suite #2
Windsor, CT   06095
860-687-1116 - phone
860-687-1062 - fax
diane@goodmanspeakersbureau.com
www.goodmanspeakersbureau.com

Du Plain International Speakers
Bureau
4201 Cathedral Avenue NW,
#1201 East
Washington, DC   20016
202-244-3338 - phone
888-387-5246
202-244-4539 - fax
jan@duplain.com
www.duplain.com

Leading Authorities, Inc.
919 18th Street N.W., Suite 500
Washington, DC   20006
202-783-0300 - phone
202-783-0301 - fax
mark@lauthorities.com
www.leadingauthorities.com

Carter Speaker Bureau
12617 Broleman Road
Orlando, FL   32832
407-384-0970 - phone
407-384-0930 - fax
clairelcarter@compuserve.com

Florida Speakers Bureau, Inc.
P.O. Box 2078
Lutz, FL   33548-2078
813-948-3222 - phone
813-948-7688 - fax
FLSpeaker@aol.com
www.FLspeakers.com

Global Connections Speakers
Bureau
4631 N.W. 31st Avenue, #166
Fort Lauderdale, FL   33309
954-972-5515 - phone
954-972-0641 - fax
globalwiz@aol.com

Speaker Gallery
P.O. Box 229
Ponte Vedra Beach, FL   32004
904-273-4622 - phone
904-273-2840 - fax
janeellis@earthlink.net

Association Resources, Inc.
3522 Habersham at Northlake
Tucker, GA   30084
770-939-9882 - phone
770-939-9883 - fax
arimgtco@aol.com

Jordan International Enterprises
P.O. Drawer 487
Roswell, GA   30077
770-992-6060 - phone
800-672-8677

SpeakerConnect USA
P.O. Box 464838
Lawrenceville, GA   30042
770-338-8388 - phone
800-377-6424
770-338-1430 - fax
speakusa@atlanta.com

WOW Solutions, Inc.
4051 Highway 78, Suite C-
102/189
Lilburn, GA   30047
770-935-9070 - phone
770-935-8777 - fax
porterpoole@mindspring.com

Burns Sports Celebrity Service,
Inc.
1007 Church Street, Suite 306
Evanston, IL   60201
847-866-9400 - phone
847-491-9778 - fax
bobw@burnssports.com
www.burnssports.com

Capitol City Speakers Bureau
1620 South 5th Street
Springfield, IL   62703
217-544-8552 - phone
217-544-1496
capitolcty@capcityspeakers.com
www.capcityspeakers.com

Joan B. Hall & Associates
2904 Scottlynne Drive
Park Ridge, IL   60068
847-825-2501 - phone
jhall@oakton.edu

Lanktree Sports Celebrity
Network, Inc.
440 North Wells, Suite 310
Chicago, IL   60610
312-755-9539 - phone
312-755-9619
novasports@aol.com

National Speakers Bureau, Inc.
14047 West Petronalla Drive,
Suite 102
Libertyville, IL   60048
847-295-1122 - phone
800-323-9442
847-367-5499 - fax
Brian@NationalSpeakers.com

Speaker Resource Center
20 North Wacker Drive
Suite 1900
Chicago, IL   60606
312-641-6362 - phone
312-641-0791 - fax
www.speakerresource.com

Agricultural/Professional
Speakers Network
10436 Oak Ridge Drive, P.O.
Box 810
Zionsville, IN   46077
317-873-9797 - phone
800-222-1556
317-873-0800 - fax
speakers@iquest.net
www.tillergroup.com

Spotlight Speakers &
Entertainment
P.O. Box 29370
Indianapolis, IN   46229
317-377-0250 - phone
317-377-0252 - fax
onstage@spotlightwww.com
www.spotlightwww.com

Excalibur International
Speakers Bureau
P.O. Box 429
Waukee, IA   50263
515-987-2643 - phone
515-987-3075 - fax
excalibur@netins.net

Winners' Circle Speaker Bureau
6602 Lafayette Road, Suite 130
Waterloo, IA   50701
319-236-9030 - phone
319-236-1515 - fax

Five Star Speakers & Trainers
8685 West 96th Street
Overland Park, KS   66212
913-648-6480 - phone
913-648-6484 - fax
fivestar@fivestarspeakers.com
www.fivestarspeakers.com

McKinney Associates, Inc.
P.O. Box 5162
Louisville, KY   40255-0162
502-583-8222 - phone
800-955-4746
502-583-2518 - fax
info@mckinneyspeakers.com
www.mckinneyspeakers.com

Program Resources
P.O. Box 22307
Louisville, KY 40252
502-339-1653 - phone
800-878-1653
502-339-8085 - fax

Signature Speakers, LLC
2200 Lake Oaks Parkway
New Orleans, LA 70122
504-282-3066 - phone
504-282-2177 - fax
nina@nwoolverton.com
www.signaturespeakers.com

AEI Speakers Bureau
214 Lincoln St., Suite 113
Boston, MA 02134
617-731-8521 - phone
617-738-0739 - fax
staff@aeispeakers.com
www.world.std.com/~lecture

American Program Bureau
36 Crafts Street
Newton, MA 02458
617-965-6600 - phone
617-965-6610 - fax
www.apb-speakers.com

Speakers Guild Inc.
78 Old King's Highway
P.O. Box 1540
Sandwich, MA 02563
508-888-6702 - phone
508-888-6771 - fax
speakers@capecod.net

Universal Speakers Bureau
121 Burcham Drive
East Lansing, MI 48823
517-351-8660 - phone
800-644-4144

517-351-3427 - fax
nancyvogl@universalspeakers.com

The Speakers Bureau, Inc.
P.O. Box 390296
Minneapolis, MN 55439-0296
612-942-6768 - phone
800-397-2841
612-941-1994 - fax
reneestrom@aol.com

Dick Hall Productions, Inc.
889 South Brentwood Blvd.
Suite 201
St. Louis, MO 63105
314-726-5200 - phone
314-726-1828 - fax
dick@dhall.com
www.dhall.com

Richard Lutz Agency
5625 îOî Street, Suite 7
Lincoln, NE 68510
402-483-2241 - phone
402-483-2746 - fax
rl94521@navix.net

Eagles Talent Connection, Inc.
P.O. Box 785
Short Hills, NJ 07078
973-376-3737 - phone
973-376-3660 - fax
etcbureau@aol.com
www.eaglestalent.com

The Speakers Network, Inc.
89 Summit Avenue, #298
Summit, NJ 07901
908-522-1610 - phone
908-522-1619 - fax

Authors Unlimited, Inc.
31 E. 32nd Street, Suite 300
New York, NY   10016
212-481-8484 - phone
212-481-9582 - fax
arlynn@compuserve.com
www.authorsunlimited.com

Greater Talent Network Inc.
150-5th Avenue
New York, NY   10011
212-645-4200 - phone
800-326-4211
212-627-1471 - fax
gtn@greatertalent.com
www.greatertalent.com

Harry Walker Agency, Inc.
One Penn Plaza, Suite 2400
New York, NY   10119
212-563-0700 - phone
212-629-7958 - fax
DonW@harrywalker.com

Royce Carlton, Inc.
866 United Nations Plaza
New York, NY   10017
212-355-7700 - phone
212-888-8659 - fax
www.roycecarlton.com

The Pros & The Cons
285 Pinney Drive, # 300
Columbus, OH   43085
614-885-0262 - phone
614-885-1712 - fax
gzfraud@bigfoot.com

Gary Good Entertainment &
Speakers Bureau
1105 N.W. 63rd Street
Oklahoma City, OK   73116
405-840-2020 - phone
405-842-5451 - fax
ggood@inervision.com

Northwest Speakers Connection
6336 Southeast Milwaukie
Avenue, Suite 800
Portland, OR   97202
503-235-1887 - phone
503-235-1790 - fax
www.northwestspeakers.com

Voices, Inc.
P.O. Box 6094
Portland, OR   97228
503-631-7477 - phone
888-962-5888
503-631-8793 - fax
francine@voicesinc.com

Premiere Speakers Bureau, Inc.
277 Mallory Station Road
Suite 128
Franklin, TN   37064
615-771-2171 - phone
800-296-2336
615-771-2177 - fax
www.Premierespeakers.com

American Speakers Association -
Bureau
32 East Rivercrest
Houston, TX   77042
713-914-9444 - phone
713-914-0944 - fax
americanspeakers@msn.com

Awesome Speakers
3243 Swandale Street
San Antonio, TX   78230-4439
210-341-4600 - phone
210-341-4637 - fax
info@awesomespeakers.com
www.awesomespeakers.com

Southwest Speakers Bureau, Inc.
17311 North Dallas Parkway
#232
Dallas, TX   75248
972-732-6100 - phone
972-732-0386 - fax
swspeakers@aol.com

Franklin Covey Company
360 West 4800 North
Provo, UT   84604
801-496-5408 x65408 - phone
801-496-5420 - fax
mchall@franklincovey.com

Speakers Plus! Worldwide
Speakers Bureau
301 Tarneywood Court
Chesapeake, VA   23320-6928
757-312-9589 - phone
800-225-2338
757-547-5753 - fax
info@speakersplus.com
www.speakersplus.com

The All-Star Agency
4829 Powell Road
Fairfax, VA   22032
703-503-9438 - phone
703-503-5823 - fax
speakers@allstaragency.com
www.allstaragency.com

The Clifford Agency
6836 Lemon Road
McLean, VA   22101
703-847-9711 - phone
703-847-9712 - fax
cliffagncy@aol.com

Washington Speakers Bureau,
Inc.
1663 Prince Street
Alexandria, VA   22314
703-684-0555 - phone
703-684-9378 - fax
info@washspkrs.com
www.washspkrs.com

Brown Bag Bookings Speakers
Bureau
2133 East Interlaken Blvd.
Suite 1
Seattle, WA   98112
206-329-3095 - phone
206-325-9609 - fax
bbbookings@msn.com

Associated Speakers Bureau
537 Wiswell Drive
Williams Bay, WI   53191
800-437-7577 - phone
262-245-6590 - fax
speakers@21stcenturyplanners.com
www.21stcenturyplanners.com

OUI Speakers Bureau
1902 Lost Dauphin Road
DePere, WI   54115
920-339-0018 - phone
920-339-0012 - fax
optionsSB@aol.com

Reckner Performance Group
4124 North Colgate Circle
Milwaukee, WI   53222
262-245-6543 - phone
800-437-7577
262-245-6590 - fax

Soldier Creek Associates
642 Gladstone Street
Sheridan, WY   82801
307-674-6268 - Phone
307-674-6278 - fax

AUSTRALIA

International Celebrity
Management Pty. Ltd.
187 Greville Street
Prahan, Victoria Australia 3181
+61 39 529 3711 - phone
+61 39 529 4573 – fax

UNITED KINGDOM

The Right Address Limited
Old Village Hall, 87 Flaunden
Hemel Hempstead,
Hertfordshire United Kingdom
HP3 0PP
+44 144 283-1314 - phone
+44 144 283-1315 - fax

Miscellaneous Contacts:

For any directory you can possibly think of go to:

www.d-net.com

Conference and Meeting Planners International
PO Box 18973
Austin, TX 78760
(512) 444-8844 – phone
(512) 444-2880 – fax
cheri@io.com

Standard Rate and Data Service
1700 Higgins Road
Des Plains, IL 60018-5605
800-851-7737 – phone
847-375-5001 - fax

Radio-TV Interview Report (RTIR)
Bradley Communications Corp.
135 East Plumstead Ave.
Lansdowne, PA 19050-1206
800-553-8002 – phone
610-259-5032 - fax

Broadcast Interview Source
2233 Wisconsin Ave. NW
Washington, D.C. 20007
202-333-4904 – phone
202-342-5411 - fax

Corporate Meeting Planners
Macmillan Directory Division
1140 Broadway
New York, NY 10001
800-223-1797 - phone

Directory of Conventions - Successful Meetings
633 3rd Ave.
New York, NY 10017
800- 266-4712 – phone
212-592-6409 - fax

National Trade and Professional Associations of America
Columbia Books, Inc.
1212 New York Ave., NW
Suite 330
Washington, D.C. 20005
202-898-0662 – phone
202-898-0775 – fax
info@columbiabooks.com

Encyclopedia of Associations
Gale Group
27500 Drake Road
Farmington Hills, MI 48331
www.gale.com
800-877-GALE – phone
800-414-5043 – fax
galeord@galegroup.com

American Society of Association Executives
1575 Eye St. NW
Washington, D.C. 20005-1168
202-626-2723 – phone
202-371-8825 - fax

Learning Resources Network
(LERN)
PO Box 9
River Falls, WI 54022
800-678-5376 - phone
888-234-8633 – fax
info@lern.org

American Association for Adult
& Continuing Education
AAACE
1200 19th St, NW
Suite 300
Washington, D.C. 20036-2422
202-429-5131 – phone
202-223-4579 – fax
drew_albritten@sba.com

FREE!

Speaker Promotional Material

Evaluation

($500 Value)

This certificate allows you to send me one piece of your promotional material for critique. This would include a short (10 minutes or less) audio or video tape, or any other single piece of your promotional literature.

I will personally analyze what you send me and send you back a customized critique of your materials along with my recommendations. Please do not send anything unless you want an extremely HONEST and FRANK critique!

Unfortunately, due to the volume of materials that I receive, I can only respond via email. I can only receive your material via regular mail. DO NOT send anything via email; it will not be accepted.

For a critique to be completed, please include all of your contact information on this form.

Name: _____

Address: _____

City: _____ State:_____ Zip: _____

Email address: _____

Please Allow 3 - 4 weeks — By Mail Only

YOUR CONFIDENTIALITY IS NOT GUARANTEED

SEND TO:

Fred Gleeck

209 Horizon Peak Drive

Henderson, NV 89012

How Can I Help You as a Speaker?

I work with a limited number of speakers every year in four primary ways. If any of these areas are of interest to you, please contact me by phone or email to discuss the rates.

One-on-One Consultation

I will sit down with you either in person or on the phone to help you create a detailed marketing plan for your speaking success. This is a one time service that comes at highly reduced rates. You cannot use this service more than once. Call the office for details and rates.

Creating Informational Products

I work with speakers to help create informational products (reports, books, audio, video, etc.) to sell at their speeches and seminars.

Presentation Skills

I also do a fair amount of coaching in the area of speaking skills. I will usually go to see a speaker at an event and give them my critique. I wouldn't suggest you ask me to do this unless you want the truth. It's tough for me to do it any other way.

Product Sales

I also do a lot of coaching in the area of improving product sales. This is an area where I can have some very significant effect on a speaker's income.

Attend a Seminar or Bootcamp/Purchase Products

See the following pages for all of my events and products.

Seminars and Bootcamps for Speakers

I periodically offer seminars and bootcamps for speakers. There are both beginning and advanced seminars and bootcamps.

The seminars are one-day events that are given at various continuing education centers around the country. One day seminars are also given a few times a year in Las Vegas and New York City.

The bootcamps are multi-day events held once or twice a year in both New York City and Las Vegas. Those held in New York take place sometime during the months of May through October. Those held in Las Vegas take place from November through April.

Both of these events are **100% unconditionally guaranteed.**

Both of these events are listed on our web site at speakingformillions.com. You can also call the office to get a list of the upcoming events.

Attend one of these events and dramatically reduce your learning curve in the speaking business. What do you have to lose? They are GUARANTEED!

Speaking Questionnaire

This pre-program questionnaire is for Fred Gleeck's presentation to ABC Corp. on 1/1/200X

We need your help! To meet the specific needs of your organization, please fill out this form as completely as possible. If you have any questions, please call: (702) 617-4205

Upon completion, please send the questionnaire to:

Fred Gleeck, 209 Horizon Peak Drive, Henderson, NV 89012

What is the Specific Purpose of this Meeting?

Type of Program: (Annual, Awards, Etc.):

Meeting Theme:

Why was this topic selected for this group?

Who Will Attend?   Male: _____ Female: _____ Age Ranges: _____

Job Titles/Categories:

Will Spouses Attend?   Children?

What takes place right before Fred's presentation?

What takes place right after Fred's presentation?

Introducer's Name:

Phone #: (   ) _____ - _____

Who are the other speakers on the program?

Speaker: Topic:

Speaker: Topic:

Speaker: Topic:

About Your Industry:

Problems?   Challenges?   Breakthroughs?

About Your Organization:

Problems? **(SAMPLE)**   Challenges?   Breakthroughs?

Is dress casual or professional?

Previous training by the group on this & related topics?

What other areas of performance need attention with this group?

What are your specific objectives for my session? What ideas do you want me to leave with them?

What would make Fred's presentation really special for the group?

Is there any publicity work Fred can do for you while he is at your event? Radio or television? Please let us know ahead of time, so we can arrange travel.

To customize the information for your group, please give me the name and phone number of three key people: (If the group will be composed of people from different levels within the organization, please include one from each of the areas.)

Name: _____ Phone:_____

Name: _____ Phone:_____

Name: _____ Phone:_____

How does your group perceive programs like this?
Favorably _____ Unfavorably _____

If you could cause those in attendance to do one thing as a result of this meeting, what would it be?

What issues (if any) should I avoid?

Any special requests that have not been mentioned?

Any additional information I should know about that has not been asked on this questionnaire?

Customer Follow-up Form

(After they agree to book you!)

Create a file for each client and staple this in the front!

Action   Date   Completed

Contract Sent out ___   Deposit Received ___

Preprogram Questionnaire Sent ___

Room Set-up Sheet ___   Microphone Needed? ___
(SAMPLE)

Preprogram Questionnaire Received ___

People Called from questionnaire ___

Customization Necessary? ___   Customization Complete ___
(SAMPLE)

Flight Booked ___

    Airline
    Time of Arrival:

Hotel Booked
    Confirmation #

Rental Car:
    Confirmation #:

Checklist of things to bring to each seminar

Overheads   Microphone

Method of transport from airport: ___

Thank you sent? Date:

Referrals Received: ___

Date thank-you note sent: ___

Letter of Rec. Rcd: ___

Follow up Program?: Newsletter, 3X or 4X or 6X or 12X a year

Speaking Glossary

Keynote - a 30 – 90 minute presentation which is usually done with no audience interaction. The primary goal of the keynote is to motivate.

Product – Any and everything that a speaker sells other than their consulting services. This could include, but not be limited to audio tapes, video tapes, CdRoms, books, etc.

Seminar – a presentation in which there is a moderate amount of interaction between participants and the instructor and among the participants themselves. It is usually an event where people are there primarily to be educated, not motivated.

NSA – the National Speakers Association is a great organization for beginning speakers to join to understand how the business works. Understand that this organization is highly political and may not serve your long term best interest unless they adopt some fundamental changes. (I'm doing my best to change it from within).

IPA – the International Platform Association is an association you should NOT join. They provide very little tangible value to speakers.

Trainer – a person who trains others in a variety of possible environments. They are not necessarily highly motivating speakers as their primary mission is to teach.

Hand Held – refers to a specific type of microphone which is held rather than attached to a speaker's clothing. Hand held microphones can be either cordless or corded.

Lav – This is a small microphone that attaches to your lapel or garment. It allows for both of your hands to be free, but doesn't allow for you to create vocal variety because you can't change the distance of the microphone from your mouth.

Demo Tape – Snippets of your presentation that are put together into a compelling 8 – 10 minute video presentation that can either be sent to potential clients directly or posted on a website to be downloaded.

Bureau Friendly – Promotional materials that are prepared in such a way that there is no way for clients to attempt to contact the speaker directly. Any indication of address and other contact information is left off.

Workshop - a highly interactive presentation where a good portion of the learning takes place as a result of the experience itself.

Pitch – That period of time during a presentation when a speaker is promoting his/her products.

Follow-Up Procedure

Contact Made: Personal, Referral, or List

Create a unique record in your database

Call organization and find out who books speakers

Talk to that person and ask questions:

> Do you ever use professional speakers?
> How often do you have occasion to use speakers?
> Which speakers have you used in the past?
> Have you booked speakers for your next meeting?

Send lit or put card into not interested file

Card then goes into one of four holders: Follow-up everyday, weekly, monthly, long-term

Contact shows interest: send more extensive info/website

Contact says yes: send contract — create a file that includes:

> Contract received
> Questionnaire Sent
> Questionnaire Received
> Staging Requirements sent
> Travel Arrangements booked
> Call 1 week before for final call
> Deliver seminar/speech
> Thank you note sent

Put temporary dot on the calendar

Contact returns contract with check - permanent dot

Deposit check and put client's name on deposit ticket

Send contact the questionnaire

Send staging requirements

Prepare any special requirements for the client

Deliver seminar

At Seminar, close for additional business and referrals

Send follow-up thank you note

Put on newsletter list

Call every 2-3 months & send articles of interest to them

Standard Introduction for Fred Gleeck

(This is exactly how I give it to my clients – but I double space it)

This introduction is customized for each group

Note: In order for Fred to properly tie in the program he is doing to the introduction, please read this introduction exactly as written.

Our speaker today has an unusual background. Born in Japan and raised in the Philippine Islands, Fred Gleeck came to the United States to go to college. He attended the University of Florida, where he graduated with High Honors and a degree in Marketing and Psychology. He then got his Masters Degree in International Management from the American Graduate School of Intl Management.

After school he moved to New York City, where Fred lived for almost 20 years. He now divides his time between New York and the Las Vegas area. In New York he owned two of his own unique businesses which received national press attention.

One was a pantyhose delivery business where he and a partner had five direct salespeople calling on customers in buildings in Manhattan. The other was a 24 hour a day, 7 day a week computer rental store chain. At one point he had three stores. Fred has real-life business experience.

In addition, he is the author of five books and hundreds of audio and video tape training programs.

Now, please help me in welcoming ... Fred Gleeck.

Seminar Evaluation

How would you rate this session in terms of content? (10 is best)

1   2   3   4   5   6   7   8   9   10

How would you rate this session in terms of presentation? (10 is best)

1   2   3   4   5   6   7   8   9   10

What Did You Like Best About the Session?

_____

_____

What Did You Like Least/What Would You Change?

_____

_____

Additional Comments:

_____

_____

May We Use Your Comments in Our Promotional Material?

If Yes, please sign here: _____

Would you be interested in? (Check if interested):

_____   One-on-One Coaching

_____   Additional Fred Gleeck Seminars

_____   Monthly Mastermind Meetings

Name: _____

Address: _____

City: _____ State:_____ Zip: _____

Email address: _____

Phone_____ Fax: _____

Sample Contract

Return to: Fred Gleeck, 209 Horizon Peak Drive, Henderson, NV 89012
If I can assist you in any way call: (702) 617-4205 or fax (702) 617-4278.

Invoice for Payment & Agreement to Engage as a speaker for:
XYZ Corp. Prepared and sent to you on: August 30, 2001

Description or Title of Event: General Session and multiple
half-day sessions Date/s of engagement: April 10, 2001

Location: Alexandria, VA

Time and Duration of Program: 1 general session (45 mn. - 1 hr.)
1 breakout session (2 1/2 hours)

Presentation Title: 21st Century Service **(sample contract)**

Further agrees to pay the following fees and expenses: $6,500 speaking fee, and the
following expenses: airfare (standard coach fare), rental car, meals, and hotel room.
All inclusive fee.

In addition, if you are pleased with your presentation, Fred will be provided with the
names of two other organizations with potential use for his services and an excellent
letter of recommendation.

A non-refundable deposit of $ 3,250 is needed to secure this date. I will give you a firm
hold on this date when this contract and the deposit are received.

Please make deposit payable to Fred Gleeck upon receipt of this invoice/agreement to
engage.

The balance: $ 3,250 should be made payable to Fred Gleeck. Balance is due at the
completion of the engagement.

Because of the potential loss of income to the speaker, cancellation of this date, less
than 90 days before the event, carries a penalty of the deposit, plus all expenses
incurred by the speaker in preparing for this date.

Special Arrangements:

Fred shall arrive at: on:

Fred needs to be available in a timely & refreshed manner for your group. Make reser-
vations on appropriate nights for Fred at:

Fred shall be transported from the airport by:

Fred shall be transported from the hotel to the meeting site by:

How long does it take to get from the airport to the meeting site?

If questions arise, Fred should contact:

An alternate contact:

Approved by   Title

Signed   Date

WEB MARKETING MAGIC. COM

Shopping Cart

The shopping cart part of this program is what allows you to perform sales on-line in your Web site. It also calculates the sale, adds the appropriate sales tax and shipping, and charges the total order to the customer's credit card.

The shopping cart appears to be part of your Web site; however, it is not. Without the customer being aware, the shopping cart zips their order to the Web Marketing Magic server and then zips back to your site for continued shopping.

Even if you do not have your own online merchant account with this program, you can still take orders and process them off-line.

How is this different or better than alternative products on the market? Most of the shopping cart systems must be installed and configured on your Web site. This requires you to purchase your own secured server certificate, which is a very expensive proposition.

With Web Marketing Magic you only need to tell us what products you sell and we take care of the rest. You literally can be up and running in five minutes.

Additionally, the shopping cart is fully integrated with the client management and marketing system and the affiliate tracking system. I know of no other program that functions like this.

Cost: Similar shopping cart programs cost approximately $1,000.

Client Management System

This is the brain of the system. It stores all of your customer information in one central database. You can search your database to learn how much total business has been done by a particular client, learn what products they have and have not purchased, and learn which of your products are selling well.

The client management system also acts very much like a contact manager (ACT or Microsoft Outlook), allowing you to make notes in a particular client file. The information can also be imported from and exported to other databases that you want to maintain. How is this different or better than other products on the market? Its uniqueness lies in the fact that it integrates with the shopping cart and the autoresponder. No other product available today can do this.

Cost: Since there isn't another product that has these functions, it would be necessary to have a programmer create the program for you. Estimated cost $3,000.

Broadcast Module

Broadcasting allows you to quickly, easily, and cost-effectively send messages to all of your customers. It can be segmented to send to any one group with the click of the mouse.

For example, you might have your database separated into two groups, those that have purchased product (publish 1)and those who are simply thinking about buying (publish 2). In other words, they have opted to be on your mailing list. You can send one message to all of the folks in publish 1 database thanking them for their order and promoting the next product. Another message can be sent tempting publish 2 list to purchase. And this can be done simultaneously, while you sleep.

How is this different or better than other products? No other system has this function.

Cost: Approximately $1,000 if it were available.

Smart Auto-Responder Module

This invaluable part of the program enables you to send follow-up messages to your clients who have expressed an interest in, or have already purchased your products or services. These messages can be sent as often as you like, with no limit to the number you can send. Messages can be sent at any time interval of your choosing.

Using this component of the system will dramatically improve your sales because repetitive, timely contact is the key to getting customers to purchase and do it more often.

How is this different or better than the others? All other autoresponders are set up on a per auto response charge. This system is unlimited and each contact is automatically entered into your database and now becomes a part of your client management system.

Because of the integration with the shopping cart, we are the only company that can automate a post sales, product specific, follow-up. Set it up once and it is done forever. That is, unless you want to change it, which is very simple and easy to do.

The main reason that this is so amazingly profound is that your ability to sell other products and services depends on how well you can target customers with specific offers based upon what they have already purchased or inquired about.

NO OTHER SYSTEM CAN DO THIS.

The advantage is that you will sell more products than someone without this system. Why? Because the process of manually managing your client and potential client base seems simple, in theory. However, it is extremely time consuming and few people do it because of the enormous amount of effort involved.

Cost: Auto responses only, about $60 per month is an average company expenditure. This depends upon how many auto responses you order each month. The management of your auto responses is unavailable anywhere and I can't begin to put an estimated cost on this.

Forms

Each customer who visits your Web site and wants to order product or be added to your e-mail list will need to provide you with certain vital information, like their name, address, etc. Forms are used to capture this customer information and until now, were a fright-filled nightmare to create.

Most form designers produce a particular type of form known as "form mail." This is a form, sent via e-mail, to you. This might be OK if you have a very limited number of responses per day. These would have to be manually entered into your database. No longer. The form is connected directly to the server containing your database and is automatically entered into your client management system, allowing you to search and send broadcast messages to a targeted audience.

Why is this different or better than other products? Very few forms are designed to integrate with your database. This saves time and we all know, time is money.

Cost: Form designers usually charge between $300 and $500 per form.

Ad Tracker

One of the biggest challenges in advertising is knowing precisely how well something works. Unlike other systems that keep track of the number of hits on your site, Ad Tracker tracks the dollar effectiveness of your online advertising campaigns.

This module is the only application that can accurately report revenue generated by your banner advertising.

How is this different or better than the other ad trackers? All others will give you data as to the number of hits you receive, but in reality that is much less valuable than knowing how many people actually buy from you as a result of a particular banner ad.

This system can be set up in a matter of minutes and requires NO technical knowledge at all.

Once again, this is the only system in the world that can report campaign specific sales revenue information from a given banner ad.

Cost: If you were to hire a programmer to write a program like this it would cost somewhere between $1,500 and $2,000.

Affiliate Module

This module will enable you to recruit hundreds or thousands of other Web site owners to resell your products for you. As discussed in this book, this is with the understanding that they will be paid a commission for their efforts, based upon their sales. What a great way to increase traffic, free, and only pay for the sales that result!

How is this different from competitors' products? It is easy to use and much more affordable than similar (although not really) products. It is the only one that is integrated with a shopping cart; therefore, you do not have to "mickey mouse" a group of software together that wasn't designed to work together. This would also call for the assistance of a programmer and that is never an inexpensive proposition.

Cost: What there is available runs approximately $1,000.

Coupon Module

Everybody loves coupons and this module enables you to create special offers on your Web site. They are great for creating a sense of urgency and scarcity. This will dramatically improve your sales.

Here is how the Coupon Module works: You create an offer like "Between now and the end of the month you get 25% off of any purchase over $100. Hurry, this offer is only good for the first 100 people who take advantage of this offer."

The system will automatically track the number of people who have taken advantage of the offer and it will prevent ordering after the passing of the expiration date. It also prohibits any orders after the specific number that you set has been reached. It will simply respond with a message to the customer, "Sorry, offer has expired. Thank you for your order."

How is this different or better? It is already integrated with the shopping cart. That means you will not have to force a coupon system to work with another shopping cart system. They already "play well together." The system will also track the total sales resulting from the coupon offer.

Cost: To create a coupon system similar to this would run approximately $1,000.

Tell a Friend

What better time to ask for referrals than when someone has just completed their order? Most people selling items on their site will have a "thank you" screen, which appears after an order has been placed. This wastes a tremendous opportunity!

Web Marketing Magic will not only thank your customer, it will ask for referrals at the same time. This enables the customer to tap into their address list and send you the names of people that may be interested in your products and services.

How is this different or better than competitive software? Well, there aren't any others. This is totally and completely unique.

Cost: A programmer could add this to your site for about $500.

EBook Module

This feature allows you to upload your PDF files and then deliver them to the people ordering from you. When an order is processed and approved (paid for), a password is generated by the system that allows the customer to download the file they have purchased. Size is not a factor. Whether it is a short report or a several hundred page e-book, you can use this module to deliver your "stuff."

How is this different or better than other eBook systems? The PDF reader does not have to be resident on the recipient's computer. The reader resides on the Web Marketing Magic server and transcribes the material as it is downloaded to the customer's system.

Cost: A comparable program would cost $500 or more.

To purchase a copy, go on-line at www.webmarketingmagic.com and sign up for a 30 day free trial. After that, you'll be convinced of the power of this program and you'll be hooked.

Profit-Building Tools for Speakers, Authors, and Consultants

If you're an author, speaker, or consultant (or aspiring to be one of these) then you must have the tools to succeed. These programs will help you maximize your chances for success. In contrast with many programs on the market, ours are filled with highly useable content that can be immediately implemented to maximize your income.

THE AUDIO SERIES:

How to Self Publish Your Own Book, Get Famous and Make Well Over $250K a Year

This one-day seminar on audio-tape will give you a great overview of the self-publishing process. It will provide you with everything you need to get started and how to develop a back-end set of products and services. You'll learn: How to quickly and easily set up your own publishing company; Dealing with publishing minutia: ISBNs, copyright registration, etc.; Tested systems to research, write and sell your book in 90 days or less; 3 simple ways to get your book written quickly; Keys to designing your front and back book covers for maximum effectiveness and much more. To learn more about this program go to www.selfpublishingsuccess.com.

How to Start and Build a Web-Based Consulting Business

If you have expertise in a topic, you can get paid for that expertise as a consultant. Most consultants spend their time chasing down prospects that have no interest in their services. This one-day seminar on audio-tape will show you the right way to prospect for high dollar customers and get paid while you're doing it. You'll learn: Your single most important asset as a consultant and how to cultivate it; Automated methods for capturing names into your web marketing system; Tips to selecting your niche to maximize your income; Understanding the funnel system and how to generate a steady flow of qualified leads and much, much more. To learn more about this program go to www.consultingexpert.com.

Marketing and Promoting Your Own Seminars and Workshops

Whether you're a speaker, author or consultant, seminars can be a very attractive source of additional revenue. There's only one problem. You can lose a lot of money if you don't what you're doing. This program will show you exactly how to promote your own events and make money doing it. I've done over 1,300 one-day events myself! You'll learn: How to select the right seminar topic and maximize your total revenue; Pricing your seminar to maximize your total revenue; Which days and months to do seminars to generate the maximum response; How to use e-mail marketing to increase attendance with a minimum of cost and much, much more. To learn more about this program go to www.seminarexpert.com.

How to Double Your Sales on the Web in 90 Days or Less

If you want to make your website successful you have to do two things. First, you have to design a site that REALLY sells. Second, you have to find an effective way to drive traffic to your site. The problem is that most people don't truly know how to do either effectively. This program will show you how to do both! You'll learn: The 3 fatal flaws that most people make on the web; What most people do backwards and how you can avoid doing them; Why it makes sense to give away something of high perceived value; Your website focus: what it should be; Creating great copy - a mandatory item; Why fancy sites don't guarantee success; What a killer sales letter is and how to write one; What kind of shopping cart you must have to maximize sales; Are pay-per-click search engines the way to go?; Myths about traffic on the internet and what you need to know now; Using newsgroups to market your site; Keys to success in affiliate marketing programs; and much, much more!

How to Make $5,000 a Day as a Professional Speaker

If you want to really make a living from professional speaking, you NEED this program. In a fast moving interview, Fred Gleeck reveals the secrets of how to get started and thrive as a speaking professional. Other programs may give you part of the story, this program gives you the whole story! You'll learn: How to develop a video demo that will get you booked 20% more often; 3 promotional tools every speaker must have and how to do them correctly; How to properly target a niche market to increase your fees and virtually eliminate your competition; Why you should never speak for "free" even though you may not be paid a speaking fee; Tips to using your own public seminars to get more private speaking engagements and much, much more. For more information go to www.speeking.com (yes, that is the correct spelling).

Creating and Selling Information Products

If you're an information marketer, you need to create information products to be truly successful. Not only will creating products enhance your image; it will also allow you to make money while you sleep. This program will show you how to turn your products into a solid money making machine that requires a minimum of effort. You'll learn: 3 ways to produce audio programs; Why you must have both books and ebooks; Key mistakes to avoid when producing your videos; Are cassettes still the way to go or must you have CDs?; Why the book is the toughest part — do that and you're 90% there; Reasons why you should never do your videos without help; Why your outline is key to your success in any information products; Maximizing your product sales at live events; Using seminars to market and sell your products; and much, much more!

24 Direct Marketing Secrets to Your Professional Services Business

If you market any service whatsoever, this is a program you can use. You'll get the inside secrets on how to do marketing that REALLY works. It's called direct marketing. It's the only kind of marketing I do. It's the only kind of marketing you'll want to do after you listen to this program. It's packed with highly relevant useable ideas. You'll learn: How to create a "Unique Selling Proposition" that will position you as the absolute expert in your field; Understanding the only 3 Ways to Increase Business in any field and how to maximize those numbers; Return on Marketing Dollars R.O.M.D. - how to increase the amount of repeat business that you generate by 30% or more; A comprehensive system to generate referrals that will double or triple your business; How to properly use the concept of a free recorded message to generate you a steady flow of qualified leads; Fully tested methods to creating expert status for yourself; Why your database is your single most important asset and how you can do it right; Tried and tested systems for generating publicity that will bring you in a steady flow of cheap, qualified leads; and much, much more! For more information on this program go to: www.directmarketingexpert.com.

How to Get Your Own Radio Show in 30 Days or Less

If you've always thought about having your own radio show, now you CAN! This lively interview format 4 cassette program will give you everything you need to have your own radio show in less than a month. Follow the steps in this program and you'll be on the air in no time. Having your radio show will allow you to promote yourself and your services in a way you'd never thought possible. This program will walk you step by step through the process. Nothing is left to chance. If you've ever wanted to be on the air, this program will show you how.

Ordering Information

Product	Price	Qty.	Subtotal
Self Publishing Program............................	$197	.... _____	.... _____
Consulting Business Program..................	$197	.... _____	.... _____
Marketing Your Own Seminars	$197	.... _____	.... _____
Make $5,000 a Day Speaking...................	$197	.... _____	.... _____
Selling Informational Products................	$197	.... _____	.... _____
Marketing Professional Services	$197	.... _____	.... _____
Double Your Sales on the Web	$127	.... _____	.... _____
Get Your Own Radio Show......................	$127	.... _____	.... _____

Package A: Any 3 items above (plus one hour consulting time)
....30% Off ... _____ .... _____

Package B: Any 5 items above (plus 2 hours consulting time)
....40% Off ... _____ .... _____

Package C: Everything above (plus 3 hours consulting time
and unlimited email support) ....50% Off ... _____ .... _____

Total: (Please add $3 per item for Shipping) ....$ _____

Guarantee: EVERYTHING we sell comes with a no B.S, money back, <u>lifetime</u> guarantee. If you're not happy, SEND IT BACK!

Name: _____

Company: _____

Address: _____

City: _____ State:_____ Zip: _____

Phone: _____ E-mail: _____

___VISA ___MC ___ Am Ex ___Personal check (payable to Fred Gleeck)

Acct No. _____ Exp. Date _____

Signature _____

(Credit card charges will appear as Fred Gleeck Productions)

Please send this form along with your check or
credit card information to:
Fred Gleeck Productions • 209 Horizon Peak Dr • Henderson, NV 89012
Phone: 1-800-345-3325 • Fax: 1-702-617-4278

Ordering Information

Product	Price	Qty.	Subtotal
Self Publishing Program	$197	_____	_____
Consulting Business Program	$197	_____	_____
Marketing Your Own Seminars	$197	_____	_____
Make $5,000 a Day Speaking	$197	_____	_____
Selling Informational Products	$197	_____	_____
Marketing Professional Services	$197	_____	_____
Double Your Sales on the Web	$127	_____	_____
Get Your Own Radio Show	$127	_____	_____

Package A: Any 3 items above (plus one hour consulting time)
....30% Off ... _____ .... _____

Package B: Any 5 items above (plus 2 hours consulting time)
....40% Off ... _____ .... _____

Package C: Everything above (plus 3 hours consulting time
and unlimited email support) ....50% Off ... _____ .... _____

Total: (Please add $3 per item for Shipping) ....$ _____

Guarantee: EVERYTHING we sell comes with a no B.S, money back, <u>lifetime</u> guarantee. If you're not happy, SEND IT BACK!

Name: _____

Company: _____

Address: _____

City: _____ State:_____ Zip: _____

Phone: _____ E-mail: _____

___VISA ___MC ___ Am Ex ___Personal check (payable to Fred Gleeck)

Acct No. _____ Exp. Date _____

Signature _____

(Credit card charges will appear as Fred Gleeck Productions)

Please send this form along with your check or
credit card information to:
Fred Gleeck Productions • 209 Horizon Peak Dr • Henderson, NV 89012
Phone: 1-800-345-3325 • Fax: 1-702-617-4278

About The Author

Fred Gleeck has been speaking professionally for more than 15 years. He has a unique background that has contributed to his success.

Born in Japan and raised in the Philippines as the son of an American diplomat, he graduated from the University of Florida with high honors and a degree in marketing. His masters degree in international management is from the American Graduate School of International Management.

Fred moved to New York City after graduation where he was promptly fired from five major Fortune 500 companies in a row. There seemed to be unanimous agreement that he should be self-employed.

His first paid speaking engagement was one of his own public seminars that he promoted via a local newspaper ad.

Since then, Fred has given an average of 100 paid presentations a year for the past 15 years.

In addition to promoting his own seminars and workshops, he has also spoken for many of the major Fortune 500 companies. They include AT&T, IBM, Hewlett Packard, and Dow Chemical, to name a few.

Fred was CareerTrack's Top Trainer for four years in a row. He has authored three books and is working on three more.

Sign up for the free tips on professional speaking by sending an email to tips@professionalspeakingsuccess.com.